A HISTORY OF

JEWISH CIVILIZATION

LAVINIA COHN-SHERBOK

PHOTOGRAPHY BY

HANAN ISACHAR

CHARTWELL
BOOKS, INC.

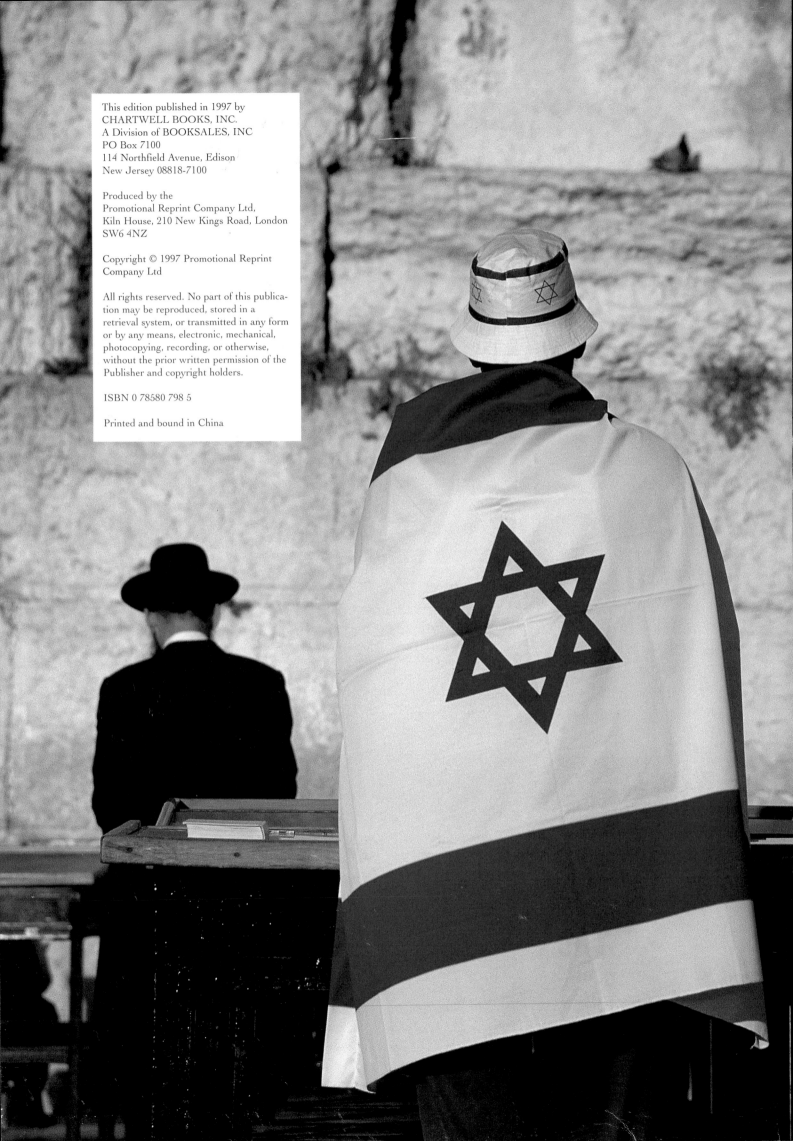

This edition published in 1997 by
CHARTWELL BOOKS, INC.
A Division of BOOKSALES, INC
PO Box 7100
114 Northfield Avenue, Edison
New Jersey 08818-7100

Produced by the
Promotional Reprint Company Ltd,
Kiln House, 210 New Kings Road, London
SW6 4NZ

Copyright © 1997 Promotional Reprint
Company Ltd

ISBN 0 78580 798 5

Printed and bound in China

CONTENTS

CHAPTER ONE
WHO ARE THE JEWS?

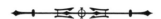

The best estimate is that there are approximately 14 million Jews in the world today. Numerically this is a tiny proportion of the Earth's population. Except in the State of Israel, which is not much larger than Wales, only in the United States, Uruguay, Gibraltar, Canada and France do Jews form more than one percent of the native population. The United States still has the largest Jewish community in the world — recent estimates place it at approximately five and a half million people. By comparison, the Jewish population of the United Kingdom is only in the region of 300,000, a very small minority group.

Yet Jews have had an impact on world civilization far beyond their numerical strength. Although the history of the Jewish people is largely a chronicle of exile and persecution, at the same time the Jewish religion has been highly influential on Western philosophy, theology and culture. Jesus himself, the founder of Christianity, was a practicing Jew. The Ten Commandments form the bedrock of modern ethical systems. The idea of the seven-day week, with its regular day of rest, is derived from the idea of the Jewish Sabbath.

At the same time Jewish individuals have made their own particular contributions. If we look at well-known Jewish names of the 19th and 20th centuries, we find a highly diverse and talented group. There is Leonard Bernstein, the composer; Golda Meir, the stateswoman; Bob Dylan, the singer; Albert Einstein, the physicist; Sigmund Freud, the psychoanalyst; Woody Allen, the movie director; Moshe Dayan, the general; Arthur Miller, the playwright; Sam Goldwyn, the Hollywood producer; Karl Marx, the political philosopher; Jacob Epstein, the sculptor; Sarah Bernhardt, the actress; Leon Trotsky, the revolutionary; Marc Chagall, the artist; Henry Kissinger, the negotiator and Helen Suzman, the anti-apartheid campaigner, to name but a few.

Despite all this talent and accomplishment, traditional anti-Semitic stereotypes survive. In the 18th and 19th centuries, Jews, as drawn by caricaturists such as Rowlandson, were seen either as hunch-backed peddlers with shifty expressions on their long-nosed faces, or as bloated rich financiers with a taste for under-age gentile maidens. The sole British prime minister of Jewish origin (he was, in fact, a member of the Church of England) was Benjamin Disraeli. Despite being a great favorite of Queen Victoria, he was invariably portrayed in the pages of the satirical magazine *Punch* as cringing, obsequious and, somehow, irredeemably foreign. This iconographic tradition has almost completely disappeared in the West, but it still persists in anti-Israeli propaganda in the Arab world.

In recent years, there has been a huge change of attitude among people of Christian background. The terrible events of the Holocaust illustrated all too clearly the result of unbridled anti-Semitism. One-third of the world's Jewish population was killed in the death camps of Nazi Europe. Since 1945 there has been a flowering of ecumenical groups. There are branches of the Council of Christians and Jews in most English-speaking countries. People from different backgrounds come together to listen to lectures on each other's beliefs, to attend each other's celebrations and to explore each other's history. As a result, real friendships have been forged between individual Christians and Jews and there is far greater mutual understanding and tolerance.

All in all the Jews are an extraordinary people. They are small in number, diverse in practice and geographically scattered. Yet despite the wide variety of culture, race and background, Jews all have a sense of belonging to one another. In a very real sense they are One People.

ABOVE: Marc Chagall was possibly the greatest of all Jewish artists. These are his stained glass windows at the Hadassah Synagogue in Jerusalem.

OVERLEAF: Celebrating the festival of Shavuoth on a Kibbutz.

Who is a Jew?

Who then qualifies as a Jew? Is a person Jewish because he or she is committed to the Jewish religion, or is Jewishness a nationality? If being Jewish is primarily a religious identification, then why do Jews speak of their peoplehood? Yet if the Jews are a nation, why do we commonly speak of the Jewish religion? Related to this question, is the issue of conversion. From early times there have been people who have chosen to become Jewish. Yet how is it possible to convert to a nationality? On the one hand there seem to be people who are born into Jewish families, but who appear to have no religion at all. Many of them, however, strongly identify themselves as Jews and also support the State of Israel. Others are deeply religious and yet seem to reject the Jewish political state. Then there are people who are born Jews, but who later join another religion — do they still qualify as Jews? And what is the status of non-Jews who have Jewish spouses and what about their children?

On the face of it, the answer to the question 'Who is a Jew?' is very simple. According to traditional Jewish law, a person is Jewish if his or her mother was Jewish or, alternatively, if they have converted to Judaism. This seems to provide clear and absolute criteria. It is generally not difficult to trace somebody's mother. Births are customarily witnessed and recorded. Technically if a claimant has a great-great-great-great-great-grandmother in the direct maternal line, even if the intermediate generations have rejected Judaism, such a person must be counted among the Jewish people. Similarly, formal conversions to Judaism can be monitored and recorded. There should be no problems.

Yet the question of Jewish identity continues to trouble the Jewish community. In this most secular of centuries, Jews have been the victims of the most appalling persecution. Yet many of those who suffered and died in Hitler's concentration camps as Jews, did not perceive themselves to be Jewish. According to Nazi legislation, anyone who had one Jewish grandparent, whether grandmother or grandfather, was forced to wear a Jewish star and was subject to dire discrimination.

Then there are difficulties with conversion. As we will see there are different branches of Judaism. Some groups do not accept the converts of other groups. Even in the State of Israel the situation is muddled. According to the Law of Return, anyone may register as an Israeli citizen if they are born Jewish or if they have converted to Judaism — provided they have not converted to another religion. So converts to Judaism, no matter where they have been converted, can qualify. Yet people who are unquestionably Jewish because they were born of a Jewish mother are turned away because they happen to be committed Muslims or Christians. At the same time, those with Jewish parents who are determined secular humanists have no difficulty in becoming Israeli citizens.

Thus we are left with our original question. Is Jewishness a national or a religious identity? There is no clear answer.

The Life of a Jew

Various ceremonies mark the stages in the life of a Jew. When the Almighty made a covenant with the first Jew, Abraham, the sign of that covenant was circumcision. Thus Jewish boy babies are circumcised on the eighth day of life. The ceremony is performed by a specialist called a *mohel*, who must be an observant Jew well-versed in the Law. The procedure is conducted formally. The baby is placed on a ceremonial chair known as the Chair of Elijah, for it is traditionally believed that the Biblical prophet Elijah is invited to every circumcision because he complained to God that "the Children of Israel have forsaken your covenant" (1 *Kings* 19.10). Then the baby's father places him on the lap of the *sandak*, or godfather (very often one of the grandfathers), who holds him during the actual operation, after which the baby is given his formal Hebrew name and a blessing is said over a cup of wine.

Medical opinion fluctuates on the benefits of circumcision. Nonetheless, it is very fundamental in Jewish culture, and even the most unobservant of Jewish families feels obliged to circumcise its sons. Sometimes, as a compromise, the operation is carried out by a surgeon in a hospital with no religious accompaniment, but it is very rare to find men of Jewish (or even half-Jewish) origin who are not circumcised.

Less ceremony marks the arrival of a Jewish girl into the world. Her birth is merely recognized by a formal baby blessing in the synagogue on a Sabbath soon after her birth.

BELOW: A Mohel circumcises a boy baby.

Among the Orthodox, even more excitement ensues if the boy baby happens to be a woman's first child. According to the Book of Numbers, every first-born male child belongs to God, and therefore the parents must redeem him back by the payment of five shekels. This ceremony, called a *Pidyon HaBen*, takes place on the 31st day after birth. The priest (a member of the Cohen class) formally asks whether the father wishes to give up his son to God or to pay the five shekels; after the money has changed hands, the father recites two formal blessings. Generally this is followed by some sort of party.

The next important life-time event is the *bar mitzvah*, or coming-of-age ceremony which, traditionally, again only applied to boys. A 13-year old boy is regarded as being a man and therefore able to fulfill his obligations under Jewish law. To mark this event, he is called up in the synagogue on the Sabbath to read the set passages for the day from the Pentateuch and the Prophets. For a child from an Orthodox family who has had a full Jewish education, the *bar mitzvah* (literally Son of the Commandment) service holds no terrors, for he can read Hebrew fluently, and has no difficulties with the text. For a boy from a secular family, it is far harder: tutors have to be employed, and preparation for the great day is a serious commitment. In modern times, an expensively lavish party often accompanies this achievement. It is not unknown to hold catered banquets for hundreds of people with several professional entertainers.

In the early 20th century, the Reform movements tried to do away with the *bar mitzvah*. The ostentation of the celebratory parties was deemed to put the community in a bad light; the practice discriminated against girls and, in any event, 13 was thought to be too young. Instead a confirmation

ABOVE: Education is a crucially important part of Jewish civilization. Here a young boy is instructed in the run-up to his *bar mitzvah*. He is wearing *tefillin*, which are leather boxes containing scrolls of sacred texts. These have leather straps attached to them and are worn either on the arm, as here, or on the head, usually during weekday morning prayers.

service was introduced for children of both sexes at the age of 16. The idea was that the entire graduating class of a synagogue religious school would prepare a service together which they would perform for the edification of their elders. Popular demand was too strong, however, and the *bar mitzvah* has survived even in the most irreligious families. Indeed, in order not to exclude daughters, a *bat mitzvah* (Daughter of the Commandment) ceremony has been devised. In Orthodox circles there are ritual objections to a woman reading from a Scroll of the Law in front of men. Non-Orthodox Jews, however, have no such inhibitions: like her brother the girl reads the set passages in Hebrew, and an equally splendid party may ensue. Confirmation has survived, but it is primarily seen as an incentive for keeping young people in religious school after the age of 13. Among the strictly Orthodox, however, it is unknown. The entire purpose of an Orthodox education is to produce men and women learned in Jewish law; they would not think of giving up their studies after their *bar mitzvahs*.

The next landmark in Jewish life is marriage. In Judaism marriage is regarded as a divine command, for the first commandment in the Book of Genesis is "Be fruitful and multiply." (There is no tradition, as there is in Christianity, of holy celibacy.) A Jewish marriage must involve two Jewish persons. Traditionally, marriage with a gentile was regarded with horror, and it was not unknown for parents to observe mourning and cut the erring child from their lives forever. Even today, with intermarriage running at over 50 percent, the vast majority of rabbis refuse to participate in any way in a mixed marriage. Wedding customs vary between communities, but certain elements are common to all. A marriage contract, known as a *ketubah*, is drawn up and is handed to the bride during the ceremony. This lists the obligations of the husband toward the wife, and indicates the dowry brought by the bride and the bride-price paid by the groom. This contract, which dates from ancient times, has given the woman protection in the event of divorce or widowhood.

Jewish weddings take place under a marriage canopy. The officiant recites a blessing over a cup of wine, and both bride and groom drink from the cup. The bridegroom then gives the bride a ring and pronounces, "Behold you are consecrated to me with this ring according to the law of Moses and of Israel." This is the act that confirms the marriage. Then seven blessings are recited over a second glass of wine, and the ritual ends with a ceremonial breaking of the glass. The origin of this final custom is obscure, but may symbolize the destruction of the Temple in Jerusalem. Weddings should be occasions of joy and feasting, while matchmaking is considered to be an honorable and important activity if the Jewish people are to survive, and a successful match is the cause of much celebration.

Divorce is to be deplored, but it is recognized that some marriages can become intolerable. If a divorce is inevitable, then Jewish law insists that the man gives the woman a *get*, a religious bill of divorce, to show that she is free to marry again. This is important because, according to the tradition, any child born of an adulterous union (that is, to a woman who is married to someone else) is illegitimate, a *mamzer*. A *mamzer* may not marry anyone except another *mamzer*, so this is a considerable civil disability. The non-

Orthodox organizations do not insist on a formal *get*, because all too often the men refuse to give it, or use it to extract an inequitable financial settlement. This, of course, means that today many Jews are technically *mamzerim* (the product of second marriages contracted without a *get*), and they therefore cannot be married in Orthodox synagogues. It is an important source of division within the community.

Women are considered to be guardians of the Jewish home and the maintainers of family purity. Among the strictly Orthodox, early marriage is the norm; birth control is discouraged, and a large family is regarded as a blessing. Among secular Jews, however, the birth rate is low. This is because today most Jewish young people of both genders go to university, pursue a professional career, marry late and delay having a family. There is real concern for future Jewish generations.

When the time comes to die, Judaism teaches that the utmost regard must be shown both for the dying and the dead. The dying are encouraged to acknowledge their sins and make amends. Once dead, the body is not left alone. It is covered with a sheet and a lighted candle is put close to its head; before burial it is thoroughly washed and clothed in a shroud. During the funeral service, Biblical and liturgical verses are chanted. A eulogy may be given, and the grave is then filled in. Memorial prayers are said, ending with the mourners' *Kaddish*, a prayer extolling the glory of God. Among the Orthodox, for seven days after the burial, the grieving family sit at home to receive visits of consolation from their friends and neighbors. During this period, known as sitting shivo, the *Kaddish* is recited every day. Then, every year on the anniversary of the death, a candle is lit in memory of the deceased, and a *Kaddish* is said by the close relations.

LEFT: Burial of Robert Maxwell on the Mount of Olives.

A Jewish wedding —
in this case a Hassidic
ceremony in Jerusalem.
Note the Chuppa
(RIGHT) — the mar-
riage canopy where the
ceremony takes place
— and the reading of
the Ketubah, the mar-
riage contract (BOT-
TOM RIGHT).

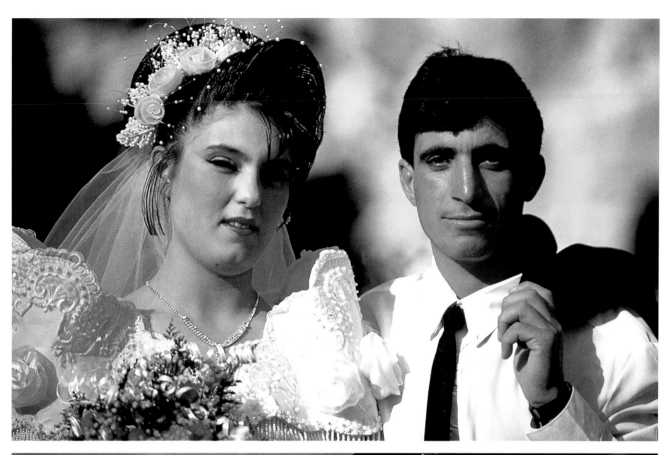

The Jewish Year

Jewish life is punctuated by regular fasts and festivals. The following largely describes Orthodox practice. A lunar calendar is followed, so the festivals fall on different days in the secular year. Most important of all is the Sabbath. According to the fourth of the Ten Commandments, "Six days shall you labor and do all your work, but the seventh day is a Sabbath to the Lord your God; in it you shall not do any work" (*Exodus* 20.9). The Sabbath, and hence the weekend, is arguably one of the Jews' great gifts to civilization. The Sabbath begins at sunset on Friday evening and continues until sunset on Saturday. During this period no work is permitted; the day is dedicated to the worship of God in the synagogue, to family life and to rest. It should be a time of rejoicing. Fresh clothes are put on; the best meal of the week is eaten; the mother lights the Sabbath candles on Friday evening to hail the day of peace and joy; parents bless their children, and it is a chance to go for short walks, to read quietly and to enjoy one's home. The Sabbath looks back to the creation of the world when God himself rested on the Sabbath day, and it looks forward to the final redemption. In a very real sense, it is a preparation for eternity.

Otherwise the year follows its regular rhythm. The New Year, *Rosh Hashanah*, takes place in the fall. It is a solemn time, the start of the 10 days of repentance. The community congregates in the synagogue to listen to the sound of the ram's horn (the *Shofar*) whose unearthly note is a call to penitence. According to rabbinic teaching, judgment is entered on *Rosh Hashanah* before the throne of God, and the verdict is sealed 10 days later on the Day of Atonement — *Yom Kippur*. The truly righteous are sealed in the Book of Life, and the hopelessly wicked in the Book of Death. But for the vast majority, people of the middling sort, there is a 10-day period of grace before their final fate is decided. Despite the solemnity of the festival, at home it is customary to eat something sweet and to wish for a "good and sweet" new year.

Yom Kippur is the most sacred day of the year; in the time of the Temple, it was the one day of the year that the High Priest entered the Holy of Holies. A strict 25-hour fast is kept and the day is spent in the synagogue declaring repentance for sin, making atonement, and asking God for forgiveness. Since sacrifice is no longer offered in the Jewish religion, fasting and repentance are the only means of making atonement. It is a long day, and it is concluded with a final blast from the ram's horn to show that the fast has come to an end. The Day of Atonement is widely observed, even by Jews who keep themselves far from the community for the rest of the year. In the state of Israel, even radio and TV stations close down.

Besides the High Holy days (as the New Year and the Day of Atonement are called), the three Pilgrim festivals of *Sukkoth*, Passover and *Shavuoth* are widely celebrated. In the days before the Temple in Jerusalem was destroyed (71 C.E.), Jews would travel from all over the known world to Jerusalem to make sacrifices on these festivals.

The Festival of *Sukkoth*, or tabernacles, takes place in the fall. It lasts for eight days (seven in Israel), and is both a harvest thanksgiving and a com-

LEFT: Rosh Hashanah — a New Year family meal

BELOW: At Rosh Hashanah the Shofar — the ram's horn is blown as a call to penitence.

ABOVE AND RIGHT: The Festival of Sukkoth, or Tabernacles, is a harvest thanksgiving and a commemoration of the Israelites' 40 years in the wilderness.

FAR RIGHT examples of the booths built to remember that time: meals are taken in them for thedays of the festival. These are in Jerusalem.

memoration of the Israelites' 40 years in the wilderness, when they lived in tents and temporary shelters and were particularly close to God. Religious Jews reconstruct that lifestyle by building a booth in their backyard, hanging it with fruit, and having their meals in it. In the synagogue, four different species of plant are bound together and waved to all four points of the compass in rejoicing. The last day is known as *Simchat Torah*, the "Rejoicing in the Law." On that day the cycle of biblical readings from the Pentateuch is finished and a new cycle is begun. The Torah scrolls are taken out of the Ark, and are carried round the synagogue in procession, accompanied by singing and dancing. Sometimes the procession even spills out on to the street and the entire neighborhood is brought into the celebration. There are many other joyful customs associated with *Simchat Torah*.

RIGHT AND
BELOW: The Feast of
Esther — Purim —
involves readings from
the book and commem-
orates the victory of the
Jews of Persia over
their persecutors.

Passover marks the beginning of the spring barley harvest, and also the liberation of the Jewish people from slavery in Egypt. The festival lasts for eight days (seven in Israel), during which time it is forbidden to eat any leavened products, thus commemorating how the Israelites left Egypt in such a hurry that they did not even wait for their bread to rise. On the first day, a Passover meal is held, which follows an ancient form during which the story of the escape from Egypt, with various commentaries, is recited. Various symbolic foods are put on the table, a huge meal (*Seder*) is eaten, four cups of wine are drunk, old prayers are recited, and traditional songs are sung. It is a major family occasion, with all the generations sitting together at one table. Traditionally it is believed that when God finally redeems the world and sends his Messiah, he will appear during the Passover season. There are few Jews, however secular, who do not remember at least one childhood Passover when the entire extended family gathered together to enjoy each other's company and to celebrate their present freedom.

50 days after Passover is the Festival of *Shavuoth*, or Pentecost. This commemorates both the giving of the first fruits to God in the Temple, and the giving of the Law to Moses on Mount Sinai. The synagogue is decorated with flowers, and the Ten Commandments and the Book of Ruth are read during the course of the service. Dairy foods are normally eaten, and it is customary to begin a child's Jewish education at this time. Among non-Orthodox Jews, confirmation is usually held on *Shavuoth*.

There are also minor festivals. *Purim*, or the Feast of Esther, takes place in early spring and commemorates the Biblical victory of the Jews of Persia over their persecutors. The Book of Esther is read in the synagogue; children dress up as Esther and Mordecai, the heroine and hero of the tale, and there is much noise and laughter. *Hanukkah*, or the Feast of Lights, occurs in the winter, very often near the Christmas period. It recalls the victory of the Orthodox Maccabees against the Hellenists who were attempting to abolish the Jewish religion. The festival lasts for eight days and on each day a candle is lit so that, on the last day, eight candles are burning. Nowadays Jewish children are often given a present for every day of the festival and there is singing and rejoicing.

Besides the Day of Atonement, fasts include the ninth day of Av, during which the destruction of the Temple by the Babylonians in the sixth century BCE and by the Romans in the first century C.E. is mourned. Less well-known fasts include the Fast of Gedeliah, the Fast of Esther, the Fast of the First-born and two fasts associated with King Nebuchadnezzar of Babylon's destruction of the city of Jerusalem.

There have been two modern additions to the Jewish calendar: Israel Independence Day takes place in the spring, and Holocaust Memorial Day soon after Passover. *Tu Bishvat*, The New Year for Trees at the end of winter, on the other hand, goes back to the days of the Temple. Particularly in Israel, people are encouraged to plant new trees, and it is a time for drinking wine and eating fruit. *Lag b'Omer*, the Scholars' Feast, in the late spring, is marked by the lighting of bonfires and picnics; traditionally, small boys have their first hair cut on that day.

So the cycle of the Jewish year is marked by the weekly Sabbath and by a variety of annual feasts and fasts. Jews lead their lives while following this pattern, with the long cycles of births, marriages and deaths. Through all the vicissitudes of their long history, these celebrations have provided a constant, recognizable rhythm which has held the people of Israel together and has kept them from disappearing among their gentile neighbors. The festivals may have grown out of historical events in the Jewish past, but in their observation they sustain the Jewish community in the present, and build up renewed confidence in a Jewish future.

LEFT: Hanukkah celebrates the victory of the Maccabees over the Hellenists who were attempting to abolish the Jewish religion.

RIGHT: Shavuoth — Pentecost — commemorates the giving of the first fruits to God in the temple.

BELOW: Celebrations for Purim — the feast of Esther.

ABOVE: Passover — The festival lasts for eight days (seven in the land of Israel), during which time it is forbidden to eat any leavened products, thus commemorating how the Israelites left Egypt in such a hurry that they did not even wait for their bread to rise. Here bakers prepare the Passover bread.

LEFT: Children celebrate Hanukkah, the Feast of Lights.

CHAPTER TWO

THE MIDDLE EASTERN BACKGROUND

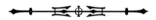

The Promise

Most successful societies are founded on myths. Rome is said to have been built by the twins Romulus and Remus, who had been abandoned as babies and nurtured by wolves. Athens is thought to have been built on the site where Athena, goddess of wisdom and Poseidon, god of the sea, held a contest for the control of Attica. Athena had caused an olive tree to grow, while Poseidon made a spring of salt water gush forth from a rock. The British have their tales of King Arthur, the once and future king, and his ideal court at Camelot. Arthur's round table may have been corrupted and destroyed by the adultery of Queen Guinevere and Sir Lancelot, the bravest knight of them all, but the dream of its future restoration lives on in the consciousness of the British people. Even a relatively new nation like the United States has its saga of the *Mayflower,* stories of the hardships of the pioneers and new colonists, the ride of Paul Revere and the tales of cowboys and Indians in the Wild West.

The Jews are no exception from this. According to Genesis, the first book of the Hebrew scriptures, the first Jew was a trader of the ancient Mesopotamian city of Ur, known as Abram. He was said to have been a direct descendant to the 10 th generation of the great Noah, who had built his ark and saved the animal kingdom, two by two, from God's wrath in the great flood. Abram, at the age of 75, had no children but was nonetheless commanded to leave his friends and relations and go with his wife Sarai to the land of Canaan. There, said God, "I will make of you a great nation, and I will bless you and make your name great, so that you will be a blessing. I will bless those who bless you, and him who curses you I will curse; and by you all the families of the earth shall bless themselves" (*Genesis* 12.1-3). Abram did not hesitate. He left his comfortable life and, in obedience to God, embarked on a series of wanderings. At one stage, to avoid a famine, he went down to Egypt where he was compelled to pretend that Sarai was his sister and not his wife in order to gain the favor of the Pharaoh. Later he and his nephew Lot split up as a result of continual quarrels between

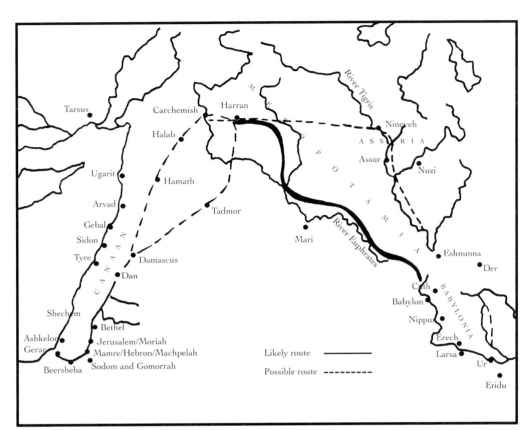

LEFT: Abraham's journey from Ur to Canaan.

BELOW LEFT: The tombs of Abraham's son Isaac and Rebecca, his daughter-in-law. Along with those of Abraham and his wife Sarah, these are in the Tomb of the Patriachs in the Cave of Machpelah in Hebron.

their respective herdsmen, and Lot had to be rescued, first from being taken prisoner by a group of marauding kings, and later from the archetypically wicked cities of Sodom and Gomorrah. In the meantime, Sarai was not growing any younger and, in order that God's promise be fulfilled, she suggested that Abram take her maid Hagar as a concubine. Hagar promptly had a son, who was named Ishmael, but Sarai treated Hagar so cruelly in her jealousy that the maid fled with her baby from the camp. Ishmael was not to be the heir of the promise but would become the father of the Arab peoples, "a wild ass of a man, his hand against every man and every man's hand against him" (*Genesis* 16.12*)*.

Then, when Abram was 99, he had another vision of the Lord. Instead of Abram, he was to be called Abraham, the father of a multitude of nations. A covenant was to be established between God and Abraham's descendants: God would give them the land of Canaan as an everlasting possession, and they would follow the Lord and be faithful to him. The rite of male circumcision was to be the token of the covenant: "Every male among you shall be circumcised, every male throughout your generations" (*Genesis*, 17.10-12). Sarai, in her turn, was to be called Sarah, and it was promised that in spite of her great age she would bear a son.

This event duly came to pass. Sarah and Abraham had a son named Isaac, and God told Abraham that it was through Isaac that his descendants would be named. The concubine Hagar and her son Ishmael were promptly disinherited and expelled from the camp, and everything seemed set fair for a happy outcome. However Abraham's troubles were not over, for God was determined to test his faithful servant for the last time. He commanded him to take his son, Isaac, whom he loved, and sacrifice him to the Lord. Again Abraham was obedient. He took the boy and traveled with him for three days to Mount Moriah (the site of the city of Jerusalem). The child was puzzled, and said, "Behold the fire and the wood, but where is the lamb for a burnt offering?" To which Abraham replied, "God will provide himself the lamb for a burnt offering, my son" (*Genesis* 22.7-8). And so the two went on toward their destination.

When they arrived at Mount Moriah, Abraham built an altar and laid wood on it. Then he tied up Isaac and placed him on the wood. Next he

Mt Sodom lies at the south end of the Dead Sea.

picked up a knife and prepared to strike. At the last moment, there was a voice from heaven. Abraham had passed the test; the sacrifice of Isaac was not necessary. Then, just as Abraham had predicted, God himself did provide a lamb for the burnt offering – nearby he noticed a ram caught in a thicket by the horns, and that was sacrificed in place of Isaac. Now God renewed his promise, declaring: "I will indeed bless you, and I will multiply your descendants as the stars of Heaven and as the sand which is on the sea shore. And your descendants shall possess the gates of their enemies, and by your descendants shall all the nations of the earth bless themselves, because you have obeyed my voice" (*Genesis* 22.17-18).

Thus, in the Jewish tradition, Abraham was the father of the Jewish people. He was the recipient of the pledge that, provided his descendants remained faithful to the Lord, they would enjoy God's blessing. They were his people, his Chosen. They would increase and multiply, and the land of Canaan would belong to them, as their rightful possession, for ever.

From Slavery to Freedom

If Abraham was the father of the Jewish people, Moses was its greatest hero. His story is to be found in the Book of Exodus, and involves many elements of the best fairy tales. By this stage in their history, Abraham's descendants had abandoned Canaan because of famine, and were living in Egypt. They were hated and feared as aliens and were put to hard labor. So frightened were the Egyptians of the burgeoning Israelite population that the order went out that all boy babies must be slaughtered at birth. When Moses was born, his mother therefore hid him, and when concealment was no longer possible, she placed him in a basket and floated him on the River Nile near where the pharaoh's daughter was accustomed to bathe. All went according to plan: the princess took pity on the baby, adopted him, and employed his mother as his nurse, and so the young Moses grew up with every advantage in the Egyptian court.

Inevitably disaster struck. One day Moses saw an Egyptian taskmaster

BELOW: The pyramids — the Israelites toiled in Egypt until led to the borders of the Promised Land by Moses.

beating a Hebrew slave; in fury, he killed the man and was forced to flee from Egypt. He settled in Midian, where he married the daughter of a Midianite priest. Then, when he was looking after his father-in-law's sheep, he had a vision of God. He saw a flaming bush, but although the fire burned fiercely, the bush was not consumed. From the bush, the Lord spoke to him. He told him to return to Egypt and insist that the pharaoh release the chosen people from their bondage. With his brother Aaron as his spokesman, Moses accordingly returned to the court. But the pharaoh was not about to lose this convenient source of free labor, and was only persuaded after 10 terrible plagues had struck the countryside: The Nile turned to blood; frogs swarmed from the river; lice ranged over the population; this was followed by a rush of flies, a cattle disease, a plague of noisome boils, a heavy hailstorm, a swarm of locusts, three days of darkness, and finally the killing of all first-born children and animals. This last punishment was insupportable to the Egyptians. The Jewish first-born had escaped after lambs had been sacrificed and their blood smeared on the doorposts of their houses. The Angel of Death had understood the sign, and had "passed over" the house, but in every Egyptian home there was mourning and desperation. The pharaoh had no choice and gave permission for the Jews to leave.

The Israelites grabbed their possessions and departed. They were in such a hurry that they did not even wait for their bread to rise, but baked it in

The Exodus of the Israelites from Egypt and their journey to the Promised Land.

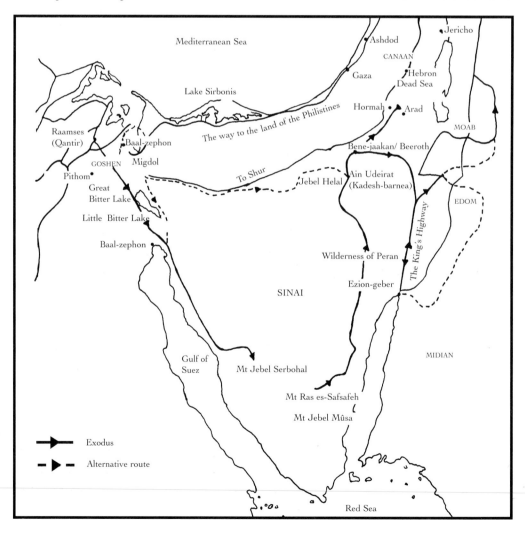

flat sheets of unleavened biscuit. After they had gone, however, the pharaoh regretted his decision. He and his chariots set off in hot pursuit, and it looked as if the Jews would be forced back into slavery. Yet Moses was equal to the situation. His ragged band had reached the Red Sea: Moses lifted his staff, the waves parted and the children of Israel crossed over on dry land. When they reached the other side, they could see the Egyptian horsemen close behind. Again Moses raised his staff and the waves crashed back into their accustomed places and in the roar of the sea the pursuing Egyptians were all drowned. The Jews were free. These are the events commemorated during the Passover *seder*.

They traveled for a short period in the Sinai wilderness, nourished by wild quails and manna which miraculously appeared on the ground. When they reached Mount Sinai (also called Horeb), Moses climbed the mountain and remained there by himself for 40 days. In the meantime, the Israelites grew restless and demanded that Aaron give them a god to worship, making him build them a golden calf. When Moses returned, carrying the tablets of the Law, he was furious at the people's idolatry. He broke the tablets, burned the calf, ground up the gold, scattered it on water, and compelled the people to drink it. Then he went back to the mountain. Again he was absent for 40 days. The people could see and hear lightening and thunder strike Sinai, and remained in terror at the bottom of the mountain. When Moses finally descended, his face shone with the light of the presence of God. He brought with him a second set of tablets containing the Ten Commandments, and, according to the Jewish tradition, the 613 written laws which are recorded in the first five books of the Bible, as well as the complete oral Law.

The Ten Commandments can be found in Exodus 20 and Deuteronomy 5. They resound down the ages: you shall have no other God before me; you shall not make for yourself a graven image; you shall not take the name of the Lord your God in vain; observe the Sabbath day and keep it holy; honor your father and your mother; you shall not kill; you shall not commit adultery; you shall not steal; you shall not bear false witness; you shall not covet.

The 613 written laws cover every aspect of life: worship, sacrifice, prayer, food, drink, clothing, commerce, and personal relationships. The Pentateuch, the first five books of the Hebrew scriptures, contains these laws; it is the essential holy book for the Jew. Week by week a section is read in the synagogue; year by year the cycle of readings is completed.

The Israelites continued to wander in the wilderness for 40 years. Moses himself did not live to enter the Promised Land; he died on Mount Nebo, overlooking Canaan, and his burial place is unknown. According to the tradition, he was the greatest of all the prophets. The rabbis taught that the entire Pentateuch had been dictated by God to him. He received the *Torah*, God's law, on Sinai and transmitted it to his successor Joshua, and this was the first link in the chain of the tradition. In Jewish legend, he is said to have been born circumcised, to have begun prophesying at the age of three months, and to have refused an Egyptian wet nurse on the grounds that he would not defile his lips which would one day speak with God. Perhaps the Book of Deuteronomy gives him the best epitaph:

ABOVE: The Jordan flows into the Dead Sea, the lowest point in the world, ten times saltier than the Mediterranean.

The Promised Land

"and there has not arisen a prophet since in Israel like Moses whom the Lord knew face to face, none like him for all the signs and wonders which the Lord sent him to do in the land of Egypt, to the pharaoh and to all his servants and to all his land, and for all the mighty power and all the great and terrible deeds which Moses wrought in the sight of all Israel" (Chapter 34.10-12).

Moses was leading his people from slavery in Egypt to freedom in the land of Canaan. It was Canaan that had been promised to the patriarch Abraham when he and his elderly, childless wife had left Ur on the promise that they would be parents of a great nation. The biblical text even specifies the extent of the country:

"To your descendants I give this land, from the River of Egypt, to the great river, the River Euphrates, the land of the Kenites, the Kenizzites, the Kadomites, the Hittites, the Perizzites, the Rephaim, the Amorites, the Canaanites, the Girgashites and the Jebusites" (*Genesis* 15.18-21). This specification covers an enormous area, and other descriptions are more modest. In the Book of Numbers, the southern boundary is described as being from the wilderness of Zin, the edge of the Dead Sea and running across to the Mediterranean Sea; the Mediterranean forms the west boundary; the northern boundary is drawn from the sea to Mount Hor, Hamath, Zedal, Ziphron and Hazar-enan, while the eastern boundary extends by the east side of the Sea of Galilee, down the River Jordan, ending at the Dead Sea (Chapter 34.7-12). Despite the fluctuating borders, in biblical times there was a clear idea of the general area meant.

It is a varied geographical region. On the west lies the coastal plain next to the Mediterranean Sea. This is flat and fertile and provides an easy line of communication between the north and the south. Between the coastal plain and the River Jordan lies the hill country. The landlocked Sea of Galilee lies to the north; south of the region of Galilee is Ephraim, and Judah is farther south still. The hill country is broken up by plains and fertile valleys, and to its extreme south lies the Negev Desert. East of the hill

LEFT: The River Jordan is born on the slopes of Mt Hermon and flows through Lake Tiberias to the Dead Sea. Traditionally, the Jordan has been the dividing line between the Promised Land and the Jews' enemies.

BELOW: The Negev Desert — not completely arid.

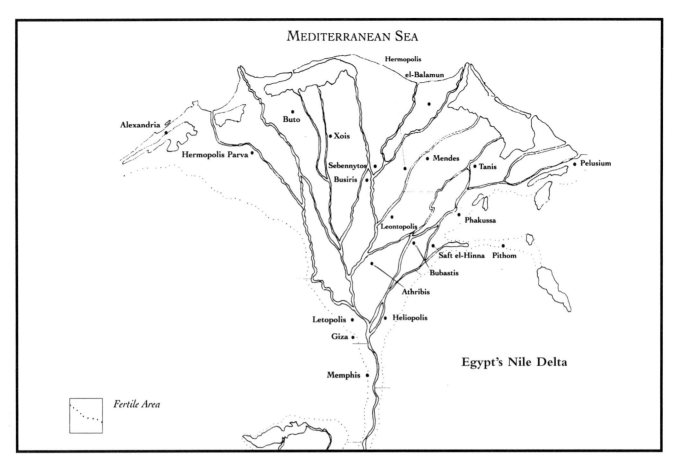

country is a great cleft through which the River Jordan flows. The river is about 200 miles in length; its source rises near Mount Hermon in the north, and it travels south through the Sea of Galilee down to the Dead Sea. This lies many feet below sea level, is extraordinarily salty, and so filled with minerals that no one sinks in it. It is surrounded by the burning-hot desert. In ancient times, farther east of the River Jordan, were the lands of Bashan, Gilead, Ammon and Moab.

Today the land of Canaan would encompass most of modern Israel, Jordan and Syria. In the third millennium B.C.E., before the time of Abraham, the great powers of the Middle East were the Old Kingdom of Egypt in the south, the successive imperial states of Mesopotamia in the east and the land of the Hittites in the north. Various independent city-states were situated along the Mediterranean coast. Commercial links seem to have been maintained between the various powers, and both Egypt and Mesopotamia competed for influence in the independent cities. The land of Canaan was also a natural corridor for invading armies; if the governments of Mesopotamia or Egypt pursued expansionist policies or waged war on each other, Canaan was all too likely to be both the cause and the site of the battles. The biblical narrative, with its mention of Kenites, Kenizzites, Kadmonites and so on, indicates that its population was of mixed ethnic origin. The Israelites, if they were to take possession of their heritage, would find themselves one tribe among many, threatened by great powers on either side, and surrounded by many competing interests.

According to the sixth book of the Hebrew scriptures, the Book of Joshua, the Israelites were not daunted. After the death of Moses, Joshua, the son of Nun, took over the leadership. Earlier, under Moses, he had been

one of the 12 spies sent into Canaan, and had described it as "an exceedingly good land . . . a land which flows with milk and honey" (*Numbers* 14.7-8). Like Moses, he led the Israelites over the riverbed of the Jordan on dry land, "the waters coming down from above stood and rose in a heap far off" (*Joshua* 3.16), and he masterminded the splendid battle of Jericho. Every day the Israelites marched around the fortified city in silence while the priests blew their trumpets of rams horns. Then, on the seventh day, they marched around seven times. On the seventh circuit the priests blew their trumpets, the people gave a great shout, and the walls fell down flat. The Israelites then swarmed into the city, took possession of it, and slaughtered all its citizens. According to the biblical story, it was a foretaste of things to come. Under Joshua's leadership, the city of Ai was taken by ambush, all its inhabitants were destroyed, and the city itself was burned to the ground. The people of Gibeon, Chephirah, Beeroth and Kiriathjearim realized that it was wiser to submit without a battle, so they were merely enslaved and became "hewers of wood and drawers of water" (*Joshua* 9.21). On one memorable day, when Joshua was fighting against a coalition of Canaanite kings, the Lord sent down great hailstones from heaven, with the result that more men died of the hailstones than were slaughtered by the Israelites. On another occasion the sun stood still in the sky to give the Israelites time to defeat the Amorites. Clearly the opposition did not stand a chance. Altogether Joshua is said to have vanquished 31 kings.

Religious obligations were not forgotten: Joshua set up an altar to the Lord on Mount Ebal, on which burnt offerings could be made; he wrote upon stones a copy of the Law of Moses, which he read to the people.

ABOVE: Another view of the bleak landscape of the Negev.

ABOVE: Detail from a synagogue in Caperneum: 'the fruits of the vineyard'.

According to the later rabbis, Joshua is the second link in the transmission of the Jewish tradition after Moses: "Moses received the Torah [Law] from Sinai and transmitted it to Joshua: Joshua to the elders . . ." (The Ethics of the Fathers). He died at the age of 110 and was buried in the hill country of Ephraim. (By then, the biblical narrative indicates, the land was conquered). As Joshua told the people in his final message:

"I gave you a land on which you have not labored and cities which you have not built, and you dwell therein; you eat the fruit of vineyards and oliveyards which you did not plant. Now, therefore, fear the Lord and serve him in sincerity and faithfulness . . ." (*Joshua* 24.13-14).

Archaeology of the Ancient Middle East

How far can the biblical tales of Abraham, Moses and Joshua be confirmed by other sources? Almost all that we know of the beliefs and practices of the ancient Middle East is derived from archaeological excavation and inevitably evidence is scant, partial, and inconclusive.

The Abraham stories probably have their origin at the start of the second millennium B.C.E. During that period the equilibrium between Mesopotamia, Egypt and the coastal cities seems to have been disturbed by waves of invasions, probably of Asiatic nomads, who are given the name of Amurru, or Amorites. These Amorites seem to have traveled through hill and desert country with their flocks and sheep, very much as Bedouin tribes do today. The memory of Abraham as a nomadic Amorite, and the story of the exodus and conquest of the land, was said at the First Fruits Ceremony recorded in the Book of Deuteronomy:

"A wandering Aramean was my father, and he went down to Egypt and sojourned there, few in number; and there he became a nation, great, mighty and populous. And the Egyptians treated us harshly and afflicted us, and laid upon us hard burdens. Then we cried to the Lord, the God of our fathers, and the Lord heard our voice, and saw our affliction, our trial and oppression; and the Lord brought us out of Egypt with a mighty hand and an outstretched arm, with great terror, with signs and wonders; and he brought us to this place and gave us this land, a land flowing with milk and honey . . ." (Chapter 26.5-9).

The first archaeological evidence of "wandering Arameans" dates from the third millennium, probably about 400 years before the time of Abraham. At Tel Mardikh in Syria, on the site of the ancient city of Ebla, a huge archive of tablets has been found. These give detailed records of the administration and diplomacy of the city, and contain a multitude of Semitic names, similar to those found in the patriarchal tales. Evidence of later invasions of the Amorites or Amurru can be found at such sites as Ras Shamra-Ugarit, Megiddo, Byblos, Jericho and Lachish. At the end of the third millennium, there are signs that these cities were completely burned

BELOW: Excavations at Jericho, one of the oldest cities in history.

down and destroyed. Then, at the beginning of the second millennium, there are indications of recovery and the beginnings of recolonization. Initially, archaeologists saw the evidence of the burning down of Jericho as confirmation of the biblical account of Joshua's destruction of the city, but in fact it is far too early: Joshua's conquest of Canaan must be placed several hundred years later.

Excavations at the ancient city of Mari show the existence of a highly successful civilization in the 18th century B.C.E. The king of Mari lived in a huge palace with 300 rooms and a vast library of tablets has been discovered there. Again, the names of the towns mentioned in these actually correspond to the names of some of Abraham's relatives mentioned in the text. It is not clear, however, whether Abraham's kinsmen had these names because they came from the towns, or whether the Abraham stories reflect current legends as to the origins of the towns.

Texts have also been found at the town of Nuzu, east of the Tigris River in Mesopotamia. These date back to the 15th century B.C.E., and describe the laws and customs of the time. This is particularly interesting for the biblical student, in that some of the customs described can also be found in the stories of Abraham, his son Isaac, and his grandson Jacob, as recorded in the Book of Genesis. So, for example, it seems to have been the practice for a man married to a barren wife to take a concubine to provide him with an heir – just as Sarah encouraged Abraham to take her maid Hagar to fulfill God's promise (*Genesis* 16). The possession of the household gods seems to have bestowed inheritance rights; this makes sense of the story of Rachel, the wife of Jacob, who stole her father's images and concealed them when she and Jacob left her father's house to return to Canaan (*Genesis* 31). Obviously it is important not to make too much of these connections; the evidence has to be taken very selectively, and many of the customs described at Nuzu have no counterpart in the Bible.

One of the most fascinating problems concerns that of the "Apiru," who are first mentioned in documents dating from the 18th century B.C.E. and appear in the Mari texts as contributing to the general confusion of the time. Their names indicate a mixed ethnic origin, and what the group members seem to have in common was a low social status; sometimes they are described as being fugitives, refugees or strangers. At Tel el-Amarna, tablets dating from the 14th century have been found. These are letters from Canaanite and Syrian kings to their Egyptian overlord, and they contain complaints about the activities of these Apiru, who are creating disturbances throughout the area. It is tempting to identify the Apiru with the Hebrews – perhaps the tablets at Mari are referring to Abraham and his wandering family, while the Tel el-Amarna examples are corroboration of the biblical stories of Joshua and the conquest of of Canaan. This solution is too neat, however.

The Apiru seem to have been a social rather than an ethnic group and, in any case, the date of Joshua's activities is uncertain. It is quite possible that the nomadic group that settled in Egypt may have had some connection with the Apiru. There is evidence in the Bible that not all the Israelite tribes had a tradition of enslavement in Egypt. If the group which remained behind as nomads in Canaan also had some connection with the marauding Apiru of the Tel el-Amarna letters, then it may have been a recognition of a common heritage which enabled the tribe emigrating from Egypt to be so easily assimilated. We can only guess.

Law and Religion in the Ancient Middle East

The archaeological findings have also added to our knowledge of the legal and religious practices of the peoples of the ancient Middle East. Several treaties and legal codes of Mesopotamia have been discovered, which show striking similarities to the laws and customs of the Jews as recorded in the Hebrew scriptures.

The oldest collection of laws found dates from the end of the third millennium, approximately 2050 B.C.E. It is known as the Sumerian Code and was drawn up by one Ur Nammu, the king of Sumer and Akkad. (The capital of Sumer, of course, was Ur, Abraham's city of origin.) In the code, the king describes how dishonest officials would be removed from office, how a system of standardized weights and measures would be established and how those who took advantage of the poor and weak would be fined. Jewish law, as recorded in the Book of Leviticus, shows the same concern with fair weights and measures: "You shall do no wrong in judgment, in measures of length or weight or quantity" (Chapters 19:35-36).

In another collection found near Baghdad, which is written in Akkadian and probably dates from the beginning of the second millennium, there is a concern with the protection of property. For example, one provision states, "If an ox is known to gore habitually and it gores a man to death, then the owner of the ox shall pay two-thirds of a mina of silver." This must be compared with the statement in the Book of Exodus:

"When an ox gores a man or a woman to death, the ox shall be stoned and its flesh shall not be eaten; but the owner shall be clear. But if the ox is accustomed to gore in the past and its owner has been warned and has not kept it in, and it kills a man or a woman, the ox shall be stoned, and its owner also shall be put to death" (Chapters 21.28-29).

The most famous of these ancient codes is that of King Hammurabi of Babylon. He ruled his kingdom, which was located between the Tigris and Euphrates rivers between 1728 and 1686 B.C.E. Almost 300 provisions have survived on a six-foot-high black tablet which was found at Susa. Many of the legal formulations follow a particular pattern: "If a man does . . . then . . ." Exactly the same formula is found in the oldest corpus of Jewish law, that of the Book of the Covenant (*Exodus* 20.22-23.33). For example, it is stated, "If a man seduce a virgin who is not betrothed and lies with her, then he will give the marriage present for her and make her his wife" (*Exodus* 22.16). Hammurabi's Code also states that the king's authority is bestowed by the great god Marduk. Similarly, the Book of the Covenant claims divine authority: "The Lord said to Moses, 'Thus you shall say to the people of Israel – You have seen for yourselves that I have talked to you from Heaven'" (*Exodus* 20.22).

It must be stressed that the Jewish law codes are by no means identical to those of Mesopotamia; they were written later and are far fuller and more detailed. None-the-less, it is clear that they emerge from a common background and social situation.

We must approach the surviving religious texts of the ancient Middle East with similar caution. Huge collections of tablets have been found in the library of King Ashurbanipal of Assyria. He ruled from 668 to 633 B.C.E., but much of the collection is far older. There is a wonderful Mesopotamian creation story, in which the great god Marduk forms Heaven and Earth from the watery corpses of the primeval gods Apsu and Tiamat, which possible gives a background to that mysterious verse in the Book of Genesis which says that before all creation, "The earth was without form and void and darkness was upon the face of the deep; and the Spirit of God was moving over the face of the waters" (*Genesis* 1.2). There is also a flood story: the Mesopotamian gods sent a great deluge to destroy humanity, and only the pious Utnaphistun survived by living in a huge boat. For those who know the story of Noah and his ark (*Genesis* Chapters 6-9), this is all very familiar.

Egyptian mythology of the second millennium is a huge subject. Most interesting, perhaps, for the student of Jewish civilization is Ra or Aten, the god of the sun. He had a secret name of power, and was associated with kingship. To his worshippers, he was very much the supreme god, the only god. Furthermore, it must be remembered that the great Jewish lawgiver, Moses, grew up in the Egyptian court, and it has been suggested that his monotheistic vision was closely connected with the cult of Aten.

The discovery of the Ras Shamra tablets at Ugarit in 1928 has added to our knowledge of the religion of the ancient peoples of Canaan. We know from the writings of the Hebrew prophets that the Jews were easily tempted to turn to the gods of Canaan. The Canaanite religion seems to have been a fertility cult which was centred round Baal, the son of the high god El (sometimes called Bull-El). Baal was the "rider of the clouds"; he sent rain to keep the land fertile and conquered the forces of chaos. When he was captured by the king of the underworld, Mot, he was rescued from the darkness by his sister, Anat, and some sort of reconciliation between Baal and Mot was then effected. This was clearly the religion of a settled, agricultural people, and it was very attractive to the Jews. When the children of Israel colonized the Promised Land after the conquests of Joshua, they were not altogether convinced that the austere desert god of Moses knew anything about cultivation. He was a supremely successful guide in the wilderness, but it was questionable whether he was equally expert at farming. The Hebrew scriptures are a record of the process by which the Jewish people finally became convinced of the total power of the One God.

CHAPTER THREE
THE STORIES OF THE HEBREW SCRIPTURES

Judges and Kings

The Bible is the major source of our knowledge of the early history of the Jews. The story of the compilation of the text and the critical questions surrounding it are complicated. For the general reader, it is probably enough that the biblical books from Joshua through the Second Book of Kings and then Ezra and Nehemiah provide a coherent record. The story begins with the conquest of the Promised Land; it includes tales of the early leaders, the judges; they are followed by the early kings, Saul, David and Jonathan; the great Temple in Jerusalem is built as a focus of the Jewish religion; the 12 tribes split into two separate groups, and the 10 northern tribes are conquered by the Assyrians and disappear from history. Then, little more than a century later, the two southern tribes are exiled to Babylon. Sustained by the prophets and the Law, the Jews keep the faith and are permitted to return 70 years later. The story ends with the reconstruction of society, a new Temple and a determination to remain the People of the Book. All in all, a period of about a thousand years is covered.

The exact date of the conquest is uncertain; some scholars argue for the 13th, and some for the 15th century B.C.E. Archaeology is not much help here either. There is some evidence of destructions in some Canaanite cities in the 13th century, but Ai, for example, which, according to the Book of Judges was burned to the ground (Chapter 8), shows no evidence of fire; The account of the triumphal progress of Joshua is probably an exaggeration. The conquest would perhaps be better described as an infiltration. At first the Israelites settled in the less controlled hill country and then, as they became the dominant element of the population, they gradually took over the cities. Certainly there is evidence, even in the biblical account, that in the early days not all the tribes acted together.

The judges, whose activities are described in the book of that name, seem to have been charismatic leaders, and appeared when the Israelites were being threatened by an external enemy. So Deborah gathered together six of the tribes against the Canaanites (*Judges* 4 and 5), although it was that splendid feminist heroine, Jael, the wife of Heber the Kenite, who finally removed the Canaanite general. It will be remembered that after being defeated in battle, the general found shelter in Jael's tent. She soothed him to sleep with milk and put a rug over him. Then, when he was unconscious, she hammered a tent peg through his temple so that "it went down into the

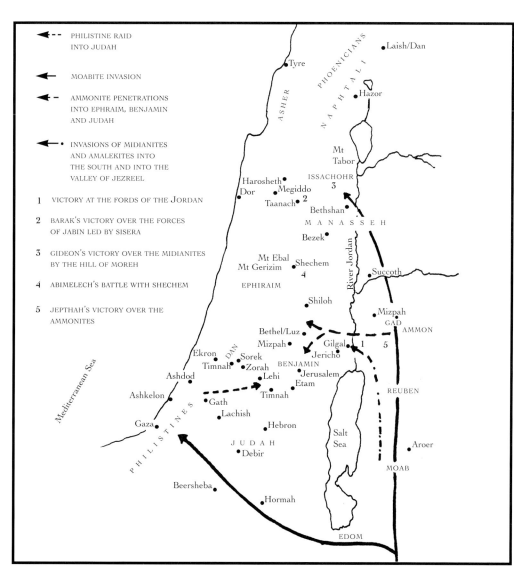

PHILISTINE RAID
INTO JUDAH

MOABITE INVASION

AMMONITE PENETRATIONS
INTO EPHRAIM, BENJAMIN
AND JUDAH

INVASIONS OF MIDIANITES
AND AMALEKITES INTO
THE SOUTH AND INTO THE
VALLEY OF JEZREEL

1   VICTORY AT THE FORDS OF THE JORDAN

2   BARAK'S VICTORY OVER THE FORCES
    OF JABIN LED BY SISERA

3   GIDEON'S VICTORY OVER THE MIDIANITES
    BY THE HILL OF MOREH

4   ABIMELECH'S BATTLE WITH SHECHEM

5   JEPTHAH'S VICTORY OVER THE
    AMMONITES

LEFT: Warfare in the
period of the Judges.

OVERLEAF:
Jerusalem under snow.
At the centre of the
photograph the Church
of the Dormition on
Mount Zion — said to
be the spot Mary 'fell
asleep.'

BELOW: Jerusalem:
looking towards the
Dome of the Rock from
Gethsemane.

ground." Of the other judges, Ehud was pitched against the Moabites (Chapter 3), Gideon against the Midianites (Chapters 6-8), Jephthah against the Ammonites (Chapters 10-11), and the strong man Samson against the Philistines (Chapters 13-16).

In those early days, there seem to have been strong feelings against having a king. At the height of Gideon's success, the people had begged him to rule over them, but Gideon had refused, "I will not rule over you, and my son will not rule over you," he had declared. Instead the people asserted their identity as a nation by meeting regularly at a central shrine where the Ark of the Covenant was kept. The Ark had been built in the wilderness under the supervision of Moses, and contained the tablets of the Law. Unlike the golden calf, it was not an idol; at the very most it was perceived as being the throne of God. Every year the people assembled together to be reminded of their history and of their obligations under the covenant. In a very real sense, their king was God.

Inevitably, firmer administrative organization became necessary. The first king, Saul, was anointed by the last judge, Samuel. His tragic story is to be found in the First Book of Samuel, *(Samuel* 9–31). Ultimately he was defeated by the Philistines and died by his own hand. He was succeeded by his young rival, the warrior David, whose exploits have become part of the folklore of Western civilization. While still a boy, David killed the Philistine giant, Goliath, first by stunning him with a stone shot from a sling, and then by cutting off his head. King Saul, in his jealousy and melancholia, tried to kill David, but with the help of his friend, Saul's son Jonathan, David escaped from Saul's court. He himself resisted the temptation of murdering Saul when he had him in his power, and ultimately it was the Philistines who destroyed the house of Saul, at the battle of Mount Gilboa. Thus, David came into his inheritance with no stain on his character.

LEFT: The monument of Absalom in the Valley of Jehoshaphat.

In the tradition, David is regarded as being the ideal king. When he was anointed by Samuel, the Spirit of the Lord is said to have come mightily upon him. He succeeded in expanding and consolidating the kingdom; and he managed to capture the city of Jerusalem from the Canaanites. As a town located between the north and the south and independent of any one tribal influence, Jerusalem was an ideal capital city. The Ark of the Covenant was moved there, a palace was built, and it became the seat of the government. David defeated the Moabites, the Edomites, the Ammonites, the Syrians, and the Phoenicians. A separate covenant was also established with him, according to the Second Book of Samuel (Chapter 7), God promised that David's house and his kingdom would be made sure for ever, and that his throne would be established for all ages. This covenant was to prove important for later Jewish self-understanding, and in the dark days that lay ahead, the promise was remembered. One day the throne of David would be restored, and all nations would turn to Jerusalem.

However, the biblical text does not portray David as being perfect – he may have been a hero, but he was not a saint. There is the colorful episode of his adultery with the beautiful Bathsheba, for example, which also involved the murder of her husband (*II Samuel*, Chapters 11 and 12). There is the sordid story of David's son Amnon, who raped his half-sister, Tamar, and was killed in revenge at a picnic organized by David's favorite son, Absalom. Absalom fled and subsequently raised a rebellion against his father, but was finally eliminated by Joab, the king's general, who, against David's express orders, stabbed him when he was caught by his long hair in a tree (*II Samuel*, Chapters 13-18). When David himself died, the kingdom was at peace, but he had failed to build a permanent shrine to the god of Israel. That task was left to his successor, his son Solomon.

The Temple

King Solomon reigned over the Twelve Tribes from approximately 968 to 928 B.C.E. He had inherited a large kingdom from his father, and he cemented his foreign alliances with diplomatic marriages. According to the biblical account, he had a total of 700 wives and 300 concubines. His wives even included a daughter of the Egyptian pharaoh, and the fact that Solomon could aspire to such a family connection indicates his political strength. Ultimately these wives were to cause trouble. They were the daughters of powerful and important men, and compromises had to be made. They were allowed to bring their foreign cults into the country, and this was perceived by the biblical writers as being a temptation to the rest of the nation.

However, Solomon is also remembered as the builder of the great Temple of the Lord in Jerusalem. It was constructed on Mount Moriah, the traditional site of Abraham's attempted sacrifice of Isaac, in the center of the city. Solomon's father, King David, had long wanted to create a permanent central sanctuary, but the prophet Nathan had told him that, as a man of blood, he was not chosen for this task, and so it fell to Solomon. The building was begun in about 964, the fourth year of the new king's reign, and it took seven years to complete.

RIGHT: Meggido was on the trade route from Damascus and Mesopotamia to Egypt and was the site of a number of significant battles — which may account for why it was chosen in Revelations as the place for Armageddon, the final battle between Christ and Satan. In reality it was an important Caananite location, saw two palaces built by Solomon and was an Assyrian provincial capital after the fall of the Kingdom of Israel.

ABOVE: The festival of Sukkoth is one of the three 'Pilgrim' festivals: times of the year that all Israelite men were supposed to go to the Temple in Jerusalem to offer sacrifices.

We are given a very full description of the Temple. It was made of the very finest materials; cedar and cypress wood was imported from Tyre; foreign artisans who were skilled in the working of stone, wood, and metal were welcomed into the country. The outer structure was of stone, about 90 feet long and 30 feet wide; the ceiling height was 45 feet. This central structure was surrounded by storerooms for the Temple's treasure. The whole was set inside a large compound bordered by another great wall – very much as many cathedrals are situated in large precincts. The compound was divided into three specific areas, one leading into the other. Furthest from the sanctuary was the Court of Women, which was designed for female worshippers, beyond that was the Court of Israelites for male Jews, and nearest the central building was the Court of Priests, for the priests who were conducting the sacrificed and leading the services.

The sanctuary itself was divided into two sections; the outer room, which measured 30 feet by 60, was on the eastern side. Entrance was through a porch from the Court of Priests, and on either side of which stood two huge bronze pillars, known as Boaz and Jachin. Inside, the walls were paneled with cedar wood, the floor was of cypress, and everywhere there was carving and gold decoration. The inner sanctum was the most holy place in the Jewish world. Called the Holy of Holies, it was only entered once a year: on the Day of Atonement, when the high priest would go in to pray for the forgiveness of the people. The walls were of decorated cedar wood, but the floor was plated in fine gold. This was where the Ark of the Covenant was kept; reputedly the same Ark that had been carried through the wilderness, and which had been kept in various sanctuaries after the conquest. It contained the tablets of the Law which had been given by God to Moses, and was guarded by two wooden cherubim.

The Temple was designed to be the focal point of Jewish worship. According to the Book of Deuteronomy, the Israelites were commanded by

God: "three times a year all your males shall appear before the Lord your God at the place where he will choose." (Chapter 16.16). These festivals were *Sukkoth* in the fall, the festival of the ingathering of the crops and the commemoration of 40 years in the wilderness; Passover in the spring, celebrating the new barley crop and the liberation from slavery in Egypt: and *Shavuoth* in the summer, thanking God for the end of the barley harvest and the start of the wheat harvest, as well as the giving of the Law to Moses on Mount Sinai. It was on these Pilgrim festivals that the Jews were to travel to Jerusalem to offer sacrifices.

In addition, sacrifices were offered every day by the priests. There were extra celebrations on the Sabbath (Saturday), on the day of the New Moon and on other festivals. The priests were male descendants of the first high priest, Aaron, the brother of Moses. The priesthood was hereditary and, in the early days, the high priest, like the king, was anointed with oil to initiate him into his office. The priests wore special priestly garments, which included a tunic, a sash, breeches and a turban. The high priest was magnificent in a gold and embroidered *ephod* (over tunic), a breastplate containing 12 stones representing the 12 tribes of Israel, a splendid turban with a gold crown and a gold, blue and purple sash.

The priests, unlike other Israelites, were not allowed to own land, and were supported by donations from the people. Divided into 24 groups, each group performed Temple duties for a week, twice a year. They offered the sacrifices each morning and evening, and they looked after the *menorah* (the sacred lamp) and the incense. They also certified and quarantined certain skin diseases (often inaccurately called leprosy, see *Leviticus* 5), administered the test of bitter waters for women suspected of adultery (see *Deuteronomy* 20 and 21) and acted as guards within the Temple precincts. Temple music was organized by the tribe of Levi. The liturgy seems to have been mainly based on the Psalms, which were either sung antiphonally between two choirs, or responsively with the congregation replying back to a soloist. The exact relationship between the priests and the Levites is not clear. All the priests were of the tribe of Levi, but not all Levites seem to have been priests. None-the-less, both groups had clear sacral functions.

The Temple and its worship proved a rallying point for the entire Jewish community for nearly a thousand years. As we will see, the original structure was destroyed in 586 B.C.E. and rebuilt in the late 6th century, rebuilt again under Herod the Great, and finally destroyed by the Romans in 70 C.E. Through all that time, it was a source of inspiration, a focus of identity, and a tangible guarantee that God had not deserted his people.

ABOVE: The Menorah, the sacred seven-branched lamp. This sculpture is by Beno Elkan. Nearly 17ft high, it can be found in the Rose Garden opposite the Knesset. It was given to Israel in 1956 by the British Government.

Kings and Prophets

In the Bible, Solomon is an ambiguous figure. On the one hand he was the builder of God's Temple, and was famous for his splendor. He was visited by the legendary Queen of Sheba (*I Kings* Chapter 10), who tested his knowledge and understanding and was impressed by his wisdom. Rabbinic legends have him the author of the *Song of Songs* and the collection of aphorisms known as Proverbs. He established strong alliances and left a secure and peaceful kingdom. On the other hand, his people were restive:

Crowds at Sukkoth.

his building program and administrative reforms had necessitated heavy taxation; his foreign wives had introduced idolatry and he even ultimately demanded forced labor from the tribes. In spite of the covenant with his father, David, Solomon had not altogether responded to the ethical demands of the God of the Israelites.

The Twelve Tribes had always been an uncertain union. For five years after the death of Saul, the 10 northern tribes had remained loyal to Ishbosheth, Saul's son, while David had initially become king only of the two southern tribes, Judah and Benjamin. Even after the two monarchies had combined, it was an uneasy alliance. Following the death of Solomon in 928 B.C.E., the southern tribes acclaimed Solomon's son, Rehoboam, as king. The northern tribes, however, made certain conditions: "Your father made our yoke heavy. Now therefore lighten the hard service of your father and his heavy yoke upon us, and we will serve you." Rehoboam replied, "My father made your yoke heavy, but I will add to your yoke; my father chastised you with whips, but I will chastise you with scorpions." Not surprisingly, the northern tribes were unhappy with this response, so, under a young military leader named Jeroboam, they rebelled against the House of David and established a separate kingdom.

Jeroboam first made his capital at Shechem, but later he moved it to Tirzah. He revived the old Canaanite shrines at Bethel and Dan to discourage his people from constantly traveling south to worship in the Temple of Jerusalem. The bull was the symbol of the Canaanite god Baal; it may have been that Jeroboam's bulls were perceived merely as being thrones for the Israelite God, but it was more likely that serious concessions had been made to the Canaanite fertility cult. Certainly the writer of the Book of Kings, who was an uncompromising follower of the teachings of the Book of Deuteronomy, was appalled. Each subsequent king of both the northern and the southern kingdom is judged by one criterion alone: either the king "did what was right in the sight of the Lord . . . and removed all the idols his father had made" (Chapter 15.11), or, as was invariably the case in the north, "he did what was evil in the sight of the Lord, and walked in the way of Jeroboam and in his sin which he made Israel to sin" (Chapter 15.34).

The northern monarchy was unstable. Jeroboam was succeeded by his son who was removed a few months later by Baasha, who ruled from 906-883 B.C.E. Baasha's son succeeded, but was murdered by Zimri, who, after a reign of seven days was replaced by King Omri (882-871 B.C.E.). Omri was highly successful politically: he built a new capital at Samaria and succeeded in marrying his son, Ahab, to the daughter of the powerful king of Phoenicia. From a religious point of view, however, this was a disaster. Ahab's wife, Jezebel, brought her own cult with her from Phoenicia, and it seemed that the religion of Baal had triumphed in the northern kingdom. Then, the towering figure of Elijah enters the story.

Prophets are mentioned in the Hebrew scriptures as part of the official religion. The young Saul had met a band of prophets after his anointing (*I Samuel* Chapter 10); King David had been both advised and reproved by the prophet Nathan. Elijah was different: he stood up against the religious

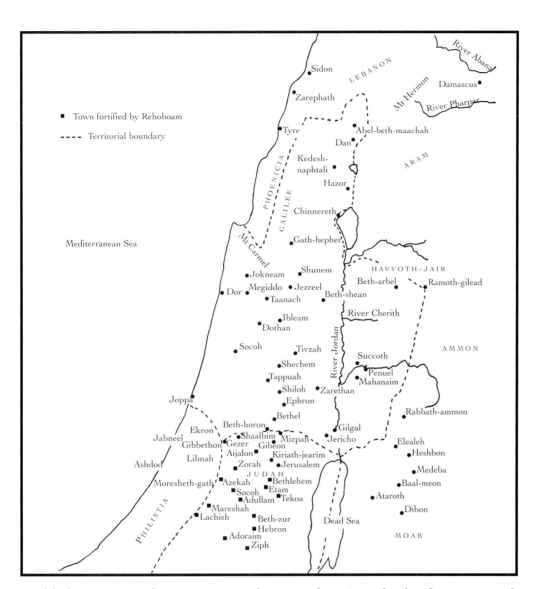

The main towns of the kingdoms of Israel and Judah.

establishment. We first encounter him condemning the land to years of drought because of King Ahab's wickedness. Then there is the extraordinary encounter between the massed ranks of the prophets of Baal and the solitary Elijah on Mount Carmel, where a contest was proposed: the first god to light the fire under the burned offerings would be shown to be the true God. All day the pagan prophets called to Baal. They cried aloud, they limped around the altar, and they even gashed themselves with lances so that the blood flowed. Nothing happened. Then Elijah came forward. He set up an altar with 12 stones for the 12 tribes of Israel, and prayed quietly to the God of Abraham, Isaac and Jacob. And the fire came down from heaven and consumed the offering (*I Kings* Chapter 18).

There are several other marvelous stories about Elijah. Ultimately he disappeared from the Earth, being taken up to heaven in a fiery chariot. To this day, Orthodox Jews believe that before the monarchy of David is re-established in Jerusalem, the new era will be heralded by the return of the great prophet. He will "turn the hearts of fathers to their children and the hearts of children to their fathers" (*Malachi* 4.6).

After King Ahab's death, and encouraged by Elijah's successor, Elisha, the throne was seized by the young soldier, Jehu. On the Black Obelisk of the Assyrian king, Shalmanezer (*c.* 840 B.C.E.), now in London's British

RIGHT: Shechem today. In Biblical history it was the site of Jeroboam's first capital.

Museum, Jehu is portrayed bowing down and offering his powerful Assyrian overlord gifts. Later the northern kingdom came under the influence of the kingdom of Syria. When independence was re-established under King Jeroboam II (787-746 B.C.E.), better days seemed to have come for the northern tribes, and it appeared to be an era of peace and prosperity. Yet another prophet arose in the land: Amos, the first of the writing prophets, preached against the people at the shrine of Bethel: "Woe to those who lie upon beds of ivory . . . who drink wine in bowls and anoint themselves with finest oils" *(Amos* 6.4,6). His words echo down to our time: "Let justice roll down like waters and righteousness like an everflowing stream" (Chapter 6.24).

In the meantime, the storm clouds were gathering both for the northern kingdom and for its poorer southern neighbor, which had remained loyal to the house of David. Under King Tiglath-Pilesar III (744-724 B.C.E.), the great Assyrian empire was stirring.

Destruction and Exile

From 740 B.C.E. the king of the northern kingdom was keeping the Assyrian threat at bay by paying regular tribute. The politics of the two kingdoms at this time were chaotic: as the eighth-century biblical prophet wrote, "Ephraim [the Northern Kingdom] is like a dove, silly and without sense, calling to Egypt, going to Assyria" (Chapter 7.11) and they "devour their rulers. All their kings have fallen; and none of them calls upon me" (Chapter 7.7). It was a time of desperate measures and shifting alliances.

In 724 B.C.E. in retaliation for an alliance made with the Egyptians, the Assyrian king invaded. Samaria, the capital of the northern kingdom, capitulated after a two-year siege. According to the Assyrian chronicles of the time, 27,000 inhabitants of the land were deported elsewhere, and other populations were brought in to Canaan. This was Assyrian policy: it was believed that tribal loyalties and affiliations could be broken down by geographical relocation. The 10 tribes of the north were scattered among the inhabitants of the Assyrian empire, and they disappear from history.

The unknown fate of the "10 lost tribes" has been the subject of much speculation. The obvious explanation is that they intermarried with the people among whom they had settled and forgot their unique religious calling. In other words, they shared the destiny of so many other groups in the ancient world: the Carthaginians, the Hittites, the Phoenicians and the Minoans, to name but a few. However, there are religious reasons for not accepting this verdict. According to the late-eighth-century prophet, Isaiah of Jerusalem, God "Will assemble the outcasts of Israel, and gather the dispersed of Judah from the four corners of the earth" (Chapter 11.12). More than a 100 years later, the prophet Ezekiel insisted: "Behold I [God] will take the people of Israel from the nations among which they have gone and will gather them from all sides, and bring them to their own land; and I will make them one nation in the land upon the mountains of Israel" (Chapter 37.22).

The belief in the continued existence of the 10 tribes was kept alive by later rabbis. The tribes were said to live on the other side of the turbulent

River Sambatyon. This steam flows so fiercely that it is impossible to cross; it does calm down on the Sabbath, but, of course, the tribes may not travel or carry burdens on that day, so they are, in effect, permanently imprisoned. Various attempts have been made to identify the descendants of the lost tribes. In the 12th century C.E. the great traveler Benjamin of Tudela claimed that the tribes of Naphtali, Zebulun, Asher and Dan lived near the River Gozan. After the discovery of the New World, it was thought that some of the Native American tribes were descended from the Jews who had escaped from the siege of Samaria, and there were unsubstantiated reports of Native American braves who spoke perfect biblical Hebrew. In the 19th century there was even a vogue for believing that the British people were one of the 10 lost tribes, and that the word "British" is derived from the Hebrew *berit-ish* (Man of the Covenant)!

Even today, Jewish communities in Bukhara and India claim to be part of the 10 lost tribes. The Falashas, the black Jews of Ethiopia, believe themselves to be descended from the union of King Solomon and the Queen of Sheba. However, the Israeli Chief Rabbinate has declared that they are members of the Tribe of Dan. In any event, it must be remembered that not all the inhabitants of the northern kingdom were taken into exile. Many of the poorest were allowed to remain and intermarried with the new immigrants. Their descendants are the Samaritans, of whom we will hear more in the next section.

Meanwhile, the southern kingdom maintained a precarious independence by paying homage to the king of Assyria; in the late 7th century, however, the imperial power was on the wane. King Josiah, who ruled in Jerusalem during this period, removed the paraphernalia of Assyrian and Canaanite worship from the Temple, reformed the cult according to the provisions of the Book of Deuteronomy, and seems to have expanded his territories. Yet with Assyria's decline, another threat emerged: The Babylonians had defeated the Assyrians in 609 and the Egyptians in 605; by 597 they were laying siege to Jerusalem itself. Initially, a compromise was reached: The Babylonians took the king into captivity, and put their own nominee on the throne.

These were troubled times. The prophet Jeremiah was convinced of the future destruction of the city, declaring: "Thus says the Lord of hosts: so I will break this people and this city as one breaks a potter's vessel, so that it can never be mended" (Chapter 19.11). He was to be proved correct. The new king, Zedekiah, plotted with Babylon's enemies, and again King Nebuchadnezzar laid siege to the city. When the walls were finally breached, all the buildings of Jerusalem were systematically destroyed. The Temple, Solomon's great temple of stone, cedarwood and gold, lay in ruins. It was an unimaginable disaster. As the Book of Lamentations puts it, "How lonely sits the city that was full of people! How like a widow has she become, she that was great among the nations" (Chapter 1.1). There is poignant archaeological evidence of the invasion. Potsherds dug up in Lachish, to the south-west of Jerusalem, contain letters written during this period. They are addressed to one Yaush, the commander of Lachish, and they described how the writer is watching out for the signals of Lachish since the signals of the other fortified city, Azekah, can no longer be seen (presumably it had already fallen.) Once the country had been subdued, the inhabitants of the southern kingdom were taken into exile to Babylon. It would be 48 years before any Jews were allowed to return to Canaan. In the meantime, they did their best to reconstruct their lives and keep the memory of the Covenant alive:

"By the waters of Babylon there we sat down and wept when we remembered Zion . . . How shall we sing the Lord's song in a foreign land? If I forget you, O Jerusalem, let my right hand wither . . ." (*Psalm* 137).

Exile and Recovery

The Second Book of Kings concludes with the destruction of the Temple by the Babylonians and the carrying off of the inhabitants of the southern kingdom to Babylon. Biblical evidence for the next period is more scanty. The major prophet of the Exile was Ezekiel, who predicted that Israel would be restored. In his famous vision of the valley of dry bones (Chapter 37), he indicated that God would bring the tribes home to the Promised Land, and would put his spirit within them. Fundamental to Ezekiel's message was the restoration of the Temple in Jerusalem:

"Behold the glory of the God of Israel came from the east, and the sound of his coming was like the sound of many waters; and the earth shone with his glory . . . and behold the glory of the Lord filled the Temple" (Chapter 42.2,5).

The story is continued in the Books of Ezra, Nehemiah, Haggai and Zechariah, which tell that the Exile was officially ended when Babylonia was conquered by Persia. The Persians permitted the Jews to return to Canaan in approximately 538 B.C.E. In fact, many chose to remain where they were: a number of the exiles had enjoyed considerable material prosperity, and within 500 years Jewish colonies were to be found in all the major urban centers around the Mediterranean Sea. Nonetheless, a small group did make its way back to Jerusalem.

The history of their return is not entirely clear. It seems that the Persians appointed a governor for Judah named Sheshbazzar in 528 B.C.E., who began rebuilding the foundations of the Temple. The task was continued by Zerubbabel, a grandson of Jehoiachin, the last king of the southern kingdom, and the priest, Joshua. The prophets Haggai and Zechariah encouraged their work. In fact, they both saw a particular role for Zerubbabel in God's scheme of things: Haggai described him as God's "signet ring" (Chapter 2.33). Yet we hear nothing more of Zerubbabel. It is to this period, however, that the beginnings of the Messianic hope can be assigned. The name *messiah* means anointed one, and the belief has remained strong in the Jewish community that another anointed one of the line of David will one day emerge, will right all wrongs, and will establish God's kingdom on earth.

Zerubbabel and Joshua did succeed in rebuilding the Temple. The new

FAR RIGHT: When the 10 tribes of the north were scattered among the inhabitants of the Assyrian empire, they disappeared from history. But to this day, people have claimed to be part of these 10 lost tribes. The Falashas, the black Jews of Ethiopia, believe themselves to be descended from the union of King Solomon and the Queen of Sheba. However, the Israeli Chief Rabbinate has declared that they are members of the Tribe of Dan.

structure was in no way as rich or elegant as the Temple of Solomon, but at least the cycle of services and sacrifices could be resumed. The Temple Mount had been a site of pilgrimage even during the exile period: not all the people of the southern kingdom had been taken into exile, and there were also some surviving descendants of the citizens of the northern kingdom. These offered to help Zerubbabel in the task of rebuilding, but their offer was spurned, for it was felt that their Jewish origin was uncertain. The problem of the relationship between the returned exiles and the "people of the land," as they were called, haunted the Jewish establishment for several centuries.

Even after the new Temple had been erected, the people remained slack in their religious observance. 60 years after the return from Babylon, the prophet Malachi was condemning his listeners for neglecting their religious duties and for marrying foreign and idolatrous wives. However, things were not allowed to lapse completely. In 445 B.C.E. Nehemiah was appointed governor of Judah; he was aided in his work by the scribe, Ezra. The precise relationship between Ezra and Nehemiah is a subject of much scholarly conjecture, but what is clear is that they shared the same objectives. Ezra himself is described as being a "priest, the scribe, learned in matters of the commandments of the Lord and his statutes for Israel" *(Ezra 7.11)*. He assembled the people together and read them the law of God, sternly calling them back to their duties.

The effect was electric. The Jews were determined to observe the Pilgrim festivals of *Sukkoth,* Passover and *Shavuoth,* as prescribed in the Torah. In addition, Ezra insisted that they divorce their foreign wives and marry only within their own group. It is possible that not everyone accepted this edict, as is illustrated in the Book of Ruth which may have been written at this time. The whole point of the book is that Ruth, a Moabite woman, a foreigner, married the Jewish Boaz, and eventually became the great-grandmother of no less a person than the noble King David. In the Jewish tradition, Ruth is seen as being the model of a true convert: as she says to her mother-in-law, "Where you go, I will go, and where you lodge, I will lodge; your people shall be my people and your God my god" (Chapter 1.16). None-the-less, Ezra won the day. Marriage between a Jew and a non-Jew has historically been anathema to the Jewish community, and even today Jewish parents have been known to observe mourning for an intermarried child, as if he or she were dead. Although the taboo has loosened in modern times, there is no question that the Jewish people owe their survival to their refusal to be dissolved into other racial groups.

The problem of the "People of the Land" remained, however. Ezra was emphatic that the inhabitants of Samaria (as the area of the northern kingdom came to be called) should not worship in the Temple of Jerusalem; they were not Jews. The Samaritans themselves, on the other hand, were convinced that they too were the legitimate heirs of the promise to Abraham and the Torah of Moses, and over the centuries they developed their own traditions. To this day they maintain that their version of the Pentateuch was the one given by God to Moses, and that their high priest is descended from the family of Aaron. Even though only a tiny community remains, they still offer the Passover sacrifice on Mount Gerizim near the modern town of Nablus. They remain one of the most interesting communities of the Jewish world.

Biblical history ends with Ezra. The present form of the Canon of Scripture was decided by a complicated process which is not entirely understood. There was no complete agreement as to which books should be included until the second century C.E. Nonetheless, the historical books stop at the end of the fifth century B.C.E. For later events we must turn to the *Apocrypha*.

BELOW: Samaritans today are convinced that their High Priest is descended from the family of Aaron. The small community still offers the Passover sacrifice on Mount Gerizim.

Samaritans on Mount Gerizim during the
Passover sacrificial ceremony.

CHAPTER FOUR

DISPERSION

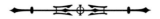

The Maccabean Revolt

Exile is a fundamental concept for the Jews. From the time of the Exile in Babylon probably the majority of the Jewish Community has lived away from the Promised Land. Nevertheless, Canaan has remained central to Jewish hopes. Even today, at the end of the Passover meal, the company declares longingly, "Next year in Jerusalem!" For the Babylonian exiles and their descendants who returned to Judah in the 5th century B.C.E., things were not easy. Because of the complicated and convoluted politics of the ancient Middle East, the land was part of one successive empire after another. The Babylonians were conquered by the Persians; in 333 B.C.E., King Darius of Persia was defeated by the young King Alexander of Macedonia. After Alexander's early death, Judah was placed under the control of the Egyptian leader, Ptolemy. Then, in 198 B.C.E., a descendant of Alexander's General Seleucus, came to the throne. This king, Aristobulus III, ruled over a large Hellenized territory.

During the 2nd century, Aristobulus and his successors tries to suppress the religion and culture of the Jews and replace them with the civilization of the Greeks. To that end, such innovations as Greek games were introduced, which involved athletes exercising and competing naked; pious Jews were appalled. Then, during the reign of Antiochus IV (who was known as Antiochus Epiphanes – Antiochus the revelation of God), the practice of circumcision was banned; neither could the Sabbath be observed nor the Torah taught. The king announced that the Temple, the rebuilt Temple of Zerubbabel, would be rededicated to Zeus, the king of the Greek pantheon; that pigs should be among the sacrifices; and that the building should be used by gentiles as well as Jews.

It was too much. Led by the priest Mattathias, the Jews rose in open revolt. After the death of Mattathias, his sons, particularly Judas, continued the rebellion. Judas was known as Maccabee, "the hammer," and the uprising was described as the Maccabean Revolt. Its history is recorded in the Books of Maccabees in the Apocrypha, and also in the *Antiquities of the Jews*, the work of the 1st-century Jewish historian, Josephus. In 164 B.C.E., the Maccabees succeeded in recapturing Jerusalem. Services and sacrifices were suspended because the Temple had been defiled; however Judas rebuilt the altar and found new vessels for the Temple services. According to the old tradition, only a tiny amount of sacred oil could be

Israel under
Hasmonean rule

Map labels:

Mediterranean Sea

Sidon

Tyre

Antiochia

Seleucia

PHOENICIA

GALILEE

ITURAEA

Ptolemais

Gamala

Hippos

Dium

Philoteria

Plain of Jezreel

Dor

Gadara

Abila

Scythopolis/
Bethshean

River Jordan

Pella

SAMARIA

Strato's Tower

Samaria

Gerasa

Appollonia

Shechem

Amathus

Mt Gerizim

Alexandrium

Joppa

Adida   JUDAEA

Philadelphia

Modein

Jericho

Jamnia

Michmash

Gazara

Jerusalem

Azotus

Hyrcania

Medeba

Ashkelon

Beth-zur

Marisa/
Maresha

Dead Sea

Anthedon
Gaza

Adora

Hebron

Macherus

Raphia

Masada

IDUMAEA

Legend:

- ■ Greek City laid waste by Jannaeus
- —·— Maccabean territory 135 BC
- ---- Kingdom of Alexander Jannaeus
- ▶ Fortress

found for the candelabrum, which was only enough for one day. Yet, as a result of God's intervention, the oil lasted for eight days, and a new festival was established to commemorate this miracle.

This winter festival of *Hanukkah* has become a popular feast, perhaps because of its proximity to Christmas. On each of the eight days of the celebration a light is kindled: on the first night one light, on the second night two lights, and so on. The lights are placed in a conspicuous place, generally by a window so they can be seen by passers-by. It is a time of rejoicing and, in some Jewish communities, presents are exchanged.

Meanwhile, the Maccabees won a period of independence for the Jewish people. They found a dynasty, known as the Hasmoneans, and even though they were not of high-priestly descent, Judas's brother Jonathan became both governor of Judah and High Priest. In his turn, he was succeeded by the last brother, Simon. Simon conquered the neighboring kingdom of Idumaea, compelling all the inhabitants to convert to Judaism, and destroyed the Temple of the Samaritans on Mount Gerizim. His sons also extended the kingdom: one conquered the northern region around the Sea of Galilee, and another occupied the region east of the River Jordan.

By the middle of the 1st century B.C.E., there was another threat on the

Hanukkah celebrates the miracle of the oil following the recapture of Jerusalem by the Maccabees.

RIGHT: Detail of a column at Caperneum with a Menorah at the top.

ABOVE AND BELOW: The Herodian was designed as a palace/fortress/mausoleum for Herod the Great. It was built on the Frank's Mount, the site of a victory by the king over the Hasmoneans.

horizon. Pompey, the Roman general, annexed Syria and turned Judah (or Judaea, as it was now called) into a client state. After a period of confusion, Herod, the son of the Idumaean king Antipater, in alliance with the Romans, laid siege to Jerusalem; Judaea became part of the Roman Empire in 37 B.C.E. and Herod was given the title King of the Jews.

Herod was hugely unpopular with the people. As an Idumaean and thus a descendant of a convert to Judaism, he was not regarded as being a proper Jew. He had the sense not to nominate himself as high priest, and tried to shore up his position by marrying Mariamne, who was a descendant of the Maccabees. He also attempted to win the favor of his people by rebuilding the Temple in Jerusalem: no expense was spared, and the final result was certainly sumptuous. Nonetheless Herod's reign was marked by plots and counterplots. He himself became increasingly paranoid: he even put Mariamne and her sons to death because he was convinced that they were working against him. He fixed up a fortress for himself in the desert on the great rock of Masada in case he was ever deposed and had to flee for his life. In fact, he died of natural causes in 4 B.C.E.and was unlamented by his people The Romans divided the land between his remaining sons, who were to rule as client kings in their father's place.

Thus, as the beginning of the 1st century of the Common Era, the Promised Land was part of the Roman Empire. The Romans were tolerant of the Jewish religion, and in general the people were not molested in their worship. Even so, after their promise of return after the Babylonian exile and their brief period of independence under the Maccabees, it was very

bitter to be under the Roman yoke. Sometimes it felt as though God's promise to the patriarch Abraham and his covenant with the great King David had been forgotten.

Jewish Sects of the First Century B. C. E./C. E.

From the writings of the Jewish historian, Josephus, we know a great deal about the Jewish sects which appeared during and after the time of the Maccabees. In addition, the discovery of the Dead Sea Scrolls near Qumran has given us information regarding one particular group, which seems to have lived in a religious community. The Christian New Testament also reflects the later part of the period: Pharisees and Sadducees are described as coming into conflict with Jesus, and there is also mention of Herodians and Zealots. It must be remembered, however, that the New Testament gives a very negative picture of Jews and Judaism. No explanation of the ideological differences between the groups is attempted, and the whole Jewish establishment is portrayed as an uncomprehending, unenlightened background against which Jesus the Messiah, the Son of God, appears. In contrast, the mass of rabbinical literature which records the discussions of the Pharisees of the time, offers a very different picture.

Let us begin with the Sadducees: the New Testament gives us a glimpse of a group of Sadducees asking Jesus a question about the fates of the dead, because they "say there is no resurrection" (*St. Mark* 12.18). The Sadducees were the hereditary religious leaders of the Jews: the high priest and his

BELOW: The caves of Qumran.

The excavations at Qumran revealed an Essene community, a monastery built on the ruins of a Judean fort. In the caves at Qumran the Dead Sea Scrolls were found in 1947 by a Bedouin. They are now housed at the Shrine of the Book in the Israel Museum, Jerusalem.

family were among their number, and they were responsible for conducting and maintaining the ritual of the Temple in Jerusalem. According to Josephus, they followed the written law as found in the Pentateuch of Moses, but they did not accept the later rabbinical oral interpretations of that law. This meant that they did not accept doctrines which are not found in the Bible, such as life after death. (In the Acts of the Apostles in the New Testament, Paul uses this fact to his advantage. When he is on trial before the Jewish council in Jerusalem, he declares, "Brethren, I am a Pharisee, a son of Pharisees; with respect to the hope and the resurrection of the dead I am on trial" (Chapter 23.6).) Because there were Pharisees as well as Sadducees on the council, they immediately started quarreling among themselves. Despite the Sadducees' wealth and prestige and their control over the Temple, they never really had the whole-hearted support of the people. They were seen as too identified with the *status quo* and too quick to make compromises with the Roman overlord.

The real spiritual leaders of the Jewish people were the Pharisees. Again, the New Testament portrays them in a most negative light, describing how they tried to trip Jesus up and criticized him for the least infringement of their regulations (for example, *St. Mark* 2.23-3.6). Josephus indicates, however, that the Pharisees had the support of many Jews. Their leaders are described as being scribes and sages, and they were essentially laymen. They were deeply involved in the interpretation of the Scriptures, and their prestige lay in their dedication to the study and development of the oral law.

To give a brief example: the fourth biblical Commandment demands that no work be done on the Sabbath. The question then arises, what exactly counts as work? After much discussion and debate, the Pharisees defined 39 different types of work. Then comes the problem as to whether a particular activity falls into any of these categories. This is where Jesus got into trouble when his disciples plucked ears of corn to eat on the Sabbath. Strictly speaking, picking any plant has been defined as harvesting – one of the forbidden types of work (See *St. Mark* 2.23-28).

Despite their disagreements with the Sadducees, the Pharisees did not wish to destroy the Temple and the sacrificial system: these things had been given by God. They went up to Jerusalem on the pilgrim festivals and they worshiped in the Temple. Nonetheless, they saw themselves as the moral leaders of the nation, the inheritors of the legacy of Moses and Ezra, while the Sadducees were the heirs of Aaron the Priest. The Pharisees were the guardians of the legal and ethical, as opposed to the ritualistic tradition of the Jews. Their platform was the synagogue, and by this time every village in Judaea had a synagogue where the people would gather to hear the Pharisees' exposition of the Law. They kept alive the hope of God's future redemption and, as the Romans tightened their grip on the country, they increasingly looked for an independent Jewish state under God's anointed king, the Messiah.

Josephus also describes the activities of a monastic group known as the Essenes. They are mentioned too by the philosopher Philo, the Roman writer Pliny, and Eusebius, one of the early church fathers. It has been conjectured that John the Baptist was an Essene. They seemed to have lived in austere communities where all property was held in common; members engaged in agriculture, but work was done for the benefit of the community as a whole. They shared communal meals and stressed the importance of moral and ritual purity. Most scholars believe that the Dead Sea Scrolls were the work of an Essene community and, from this material, we have a full picture of the organization and beliefs of the group. They seem to have been inspired by a vision of the last days of the world, which they were convinced were soon to dawn. They believed themselves to be the faithful remnant, the last of the righteous of Israel, and they thought of both the Pharisees and the Sadducees as corrupt compromisers.

The other two groups mentioned in the New Testament were essentially political. The Herodians supported the rule of the puppet-king, Herod Antipas, the son of Herod the Great. In contrast, the Zealots were freedom-fighters who detested the Roman Empire and all its works. Jesus seems to have numbered a Zealot, Simon, among his 12 close disciples. At this period, the supreme religious body of the Jews was the Sanhedrin, the council. This was composed of both the Pharisees and Sadducees, and is mentioned in the New Testament (both Jesus and Paul were tried in front of the Sanhedrin.) However, scholars disagree as to its exact nature and religious function. Its two senior officials were known as the *Nasi* [prince], and the *Av Bet Din* [father of the court].

The Jewish War

The magnificent Temple built by King Herod is no longer standing; all that remains of it is the vast Wailing (Western) Wall. This is the most sacred place in the Jewish world, and every year thousands of Jews make a pilgrimage to stand by it, to touch it and to say their prayers by it. It is a huge structure, and it gives some idea of the grandeur of the original building. How then did it come to be destroyed?

LEFT and OVERLEAF: All that remains of Herod the Great's temple is the Western Wall — the Wailing Wall, the most sacred place in the Jewish world.

Herod himself died in 4 B.C.E., and his kingdom was divided by the Romans between his three surviving sons. 10 years later, one of the three, Archaelus, was sent into exile, and his portion, the old kingdom of Judaea, became a Roman province, ruled over by a procurator; the Jews detested this arrangement. This was why some of the inhabitants of the north, who were still ruled over by Herod Antipas, supported the government and were known as Herodians. Many Roman customs were offensive to the Jews. For example, the Romans periodically made censuses of their subject peoples; this was contrary to Jewish law. During this period there are records of several small-scale Messianic movements, of which the cult of Jesus of Nazareth was the most famous. Of all the procurators, Pontius Pilate, who plays an important part in the New Testament, was particularly insensitive to Jewish ways. He brought the Roman standards with the emperor's insignia into the Holy City and used the Temple funds to pay for a new aqueduct.During the reign of the Emperor Claudius (C.E. 41-54), there was a short respite. Judaea again became a self-governing client state under the kingship of Herod Agrippa, but on King Agrippa's death in C.E. 44, the country again became a province. It was an unquiet time: the rich and the poor were hostile to one another; the countryside was full of roaming prophets and holy men. Between C.E. 46 and 48, there was a terrible famine, the poor starved, and there was a heightened sense of Messianic

Jerusalem and the Second Temple.

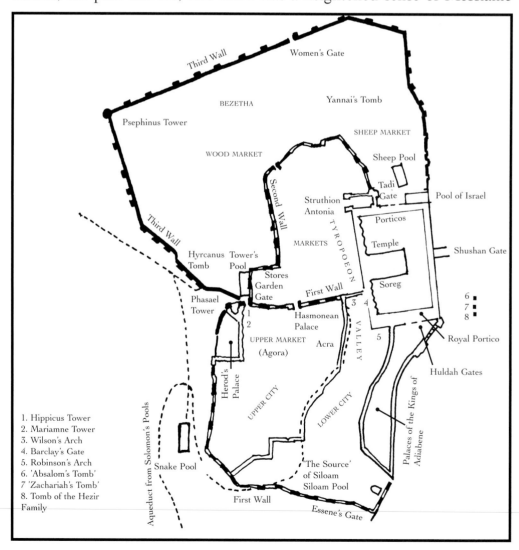

1. Hippicus Tower
2. Mariamne Tower
3. Wilson's Arch
4. Barclay's Gate
5. Robinson's Arch
6. 'Absalom's Tomb'
7. 'Zachariah's Tomb'
8. Tomb of the Hezir Family

LEFT: A model reconstruction of the walls of the Second (Herodian) Temple.

excitement. The Zealot party became increasingly influential, and the historian Josephus describes how the Zealots were not only fanatical freedom-fighters against the Romans, they were also profoundly religious. They were dedicated to God, they kept the laws of the Torah, and were determined to establish God's kingdom on earth as soon as possible; they saw as blasphemy and sacrilege the presence of the pagan Romans in the Promised Land. Meanwhile, the Sadducees continued to try to make compromises with the occupying power, but the later procurators were men of little sympathy, who continually outraged Jewish religious feeling. In general, the Pharisees were men of peace, but the people could not be held in check for ever.

Things exploded in C.E. 66. In a popular uprising, a Roman legion was destroyed by a group of Zealots. The Roman governor reacted at once and marched on the city of Jerusalem, but the rebels had overthrown the government and were in control. The Roman general, Vespasian, brought in additional troops from the north, put the fortress of Jotapata under siege, and gradually subjugated Idumaea, western Judea, Samaria, and Jericho. Vespasian's son, Titus, was put in charge of the siege of Jerusalem and Josephus's *Jewish War* gives us an almost blow-by-blow account of the conflict. By the end of May C.E. 70, the newer part of the city was under Roman control; by late July the Romans had captured the citadel next to the Temple; on August 6 C.E. 70 the daily sacrifices were suspended; and on August 28 the Temple was set alight. According to Josephus, Titus himself wanted to save the Temple, but the fire was started by a single soldier hurling a torch into the building, and the other troops enthusiastically followed his example. The great Temple was thus burnt to the ground; only the western wall survived.

BELOW: Titus commemorated the successful despatch of the C. E. 70 revolt by building his eponymous arch in Rome.

In accordance with Roman custom, Vespasian and Titus led a procession of Triumph through Rome after the victory. Prisoners taken in the siege were dragged along in chains behind the chariots, and the various ceremonial objects looted during the siege were also displayed. The Arch of Titus was built in Rome to commemorate the occasion and the frieze of the arch clearly shows Roman soldiers carrying the great seven-branch candelabrum of the Temple.

However, Judaea had not been completely subdued. A group of Zealots had fled southward, and had taken possession of King Herod's old bolthole, the fortress of Masada near the Dead Sea. Only small numbers of resisters were involved, but the Romans could not allow their prestige to be destroyed by a few defiant rebels. They therefore laid siege to Masada and eventually it fell in C.E. 74. Josephus vividly describes the end of the Zealots who, on the eve of the final battle, chose to commit suicide rather than fall into the hands of the enemy. Their leader's speech is worth quoting:

"While we are free and masters of our swords, let us make a glorious use of them and preserve our liberties. Let us die as free men, with the comfort and company of our wives and children about us. It is but what they themselves desire, what our laws require at our hands, and what Providence itself has made necessary for us. Only the Romans are against it, for fear we should do their work for them. Let us dispatch then, for it will be to our immortal honor to take the prize they long for out of their hands, in leaving them only the poor satisfaction of dead bodies for their triumph."

The Zealots are regarded as heroic figure in Jewish history. Furthermore, since the founding of the state of Israel in 1948, the Israeli government and the world-wide Jewish community have been determined that Masada will not fall again.

ABOVE LEFT and ABOVE: Masada —
this formidable Herodian fortress would
take all the might of the Roman Army to
subdue. They built a huge ramp to the top
but the Zealots preferred suicide to capture.

The Synagogue

The Temple had been destroyed. There could be no more sacrifices, since the Book of Deuteronomy makes it clear that sacrifice is only permitted in one place, there was no longer any point in traveling three times a year to the Holy City. The Sadducees had no more regular priestly duties to fulfill; there was no Holy of Holies for the high priest to enter once a year on the Day of Atonement. The altars were cast down; the sacred vessels had been looted. The Ark of the Covenant, holding the very tablets given by God to Moses on Mount Sinai had either been destroyed in the flames or was buried under thousands of tons of rubble. It was an unimaginable catastrophe which surely demonstrated that God had finally deserted his people. Yet the Jewish people and the Jewish religion survived. That they did so was largely due to a single institution – the synagogue.

The origin of the synagogue is obscure, but it probably goes back to the time of the exile in Babylon in the 6th century B.C.E. – another era when the Temple of God in Jerusalem lay in ruins. In the Book of Ezekiel, there is a hint that God has provided another sanctuary for the people in their dispersion (See Chapter 11.16). This verse was widely understood by the later rabbis to be referring to the synagogue. The exiles seem to have met together on a regular basis to say their prayers, to listen to readings from the Scriptures, and to hear expositions of the sacred texts. Because no sacrifices could be offered, there was no role for priests or Levites: any Jew could stand up to read from the Torah or the Books of Prophecy, and lead the congregation in prayer. The synagogue became not only a house of worship, but a community facility, a debating chamber, a place of study and a resource center. Although we have little firm evidence about its development as an institution, there is archaeological evidence that synagogues were being built in the villages in the Holy Land, as well as in most significant urban centers around the Mediterranean Sea by the 1st century C.E.

The New Testament provides interesting glimpses of village and town synagogues. We are told that, after Jesus's sojourn in the wilderness, he returned to the town of Nazareth where he had been brought up:

"And he went to the synagogue as his custom was, on the Sabbath day. And he stood up to read; and there was given to him the Book of the Prophet Isaiah. He opened the book and found the place where it is written: The Spirit of the Lord is upon me . . . And he closed the book and gave it back to the attendant and sat down; and the eyes of all in the synagogue were fixed on him. And he began to say them, 'Today this Scripture has been fulfilled in your hearing . .' ." (*St. Luke*, Chapter 4.16-21).

Here we have the layman Jesus standing up to read from the Scriptures on the Sabbath Day and then expounding the meaning of the text.

The apostle Paul was also a regular attender at synagogue. In fact, he used the synagogue network to provide new contacts in strange cities as he preached the Christian gospel around the urban centers of the eastern Mediterranean. On his second missionary journey, for example, the Acts of

The Temple had been destroyed: the Ark of the Covenant lost. Henceforth the synagogue would become the focal point for Jewish religious life.

LEFT: The Ben Zakai synagogue in the Old City of Jerusalem.

BELOW: Here a representation of the chest holding the Torah from the ruins of the 4th century synagogue at Caperneum.

Ancient synagogues at Masada (ABOVE), Korazim (RIGHT) and the Chabad Lubawitch Synagogue in Jerusalem's Old City (FAR RIGHT).

the Apostles records that he preached in the synagogues of Philippi, Thessalonica (where we are told that he "went in as was his custom and for three weeks he argued with them from the Scriptures"), Beroea, Athens, Corinth and Ephesus.

With the destruction of the Temple in C.E. 70, the synagogue became the central institution of communal Jewish life. Many of the rituals of the Temple were modified and adopted for synagogue use. And although there could no longer be sacrifices, there could be regular prayer services three times a day to correspond with the morning, afternoon and evening offerings. Priests were no longer necessary, but the synagogue ritual required a quorum of 10 adult Jewish men, and any male could read the Torah to the congregation. Women were given separate (and generally out-of-the-way) seating, as in the Temple in Jerusalem. The central ritual object could no longer be the Ark of the Covenant, made under God's instructions and carrying Moses's tablets of the Law; instead it was the Ark, a cabinet built into the nearest wall to Jerusalem, which contained the handwritten scrolls of the Pentateuch. A sacred lamp could still burn before it and before the Ark was also placed the *bimah,* the raised platform from which all reading and exposition took place.

Over the centuries, synagogue architecture has varied according to the fashions of the host nations. In modern times there have been wooden synagogue in Poland, brick and stone buildings throughout Europe, and magnificent structures in Spain and North Africa, which have been influenced by the Moorish tradition of architecture. The great synagogues built for the 17th-century Jewish communities in Amsterdam are large, airy buildings with splendid furnishings, while the 20th-century synagogues of the United States are the product of the commissioning of innovative modernist architects by an affluent and successful religious group.

Despite the variety of their external designs, the functions of the synagogue has not changed since the time of the Exile, although in modern Reform communities there is no need for a separate women's section: men and women sit together. (The Orthodox Jews, however, have retained the old customs.) The synagogue remains the place where Jews can meet, study, and pray. Throughout the long eras of misunderstanding, exile, and persecution, the synagogue has provided a haven of Jewishness in a largely hostile, gentile world.

Dispersion

Judaea was not subdued by the war of C.E. 70, and in C.E. 132 another Messianic figure emerged. According to the Book of Numbers (Chapter 24, verse 17), "there shall step forth a star out of Jacob"; Simeon bar Kokhba, whose name means "son of a star," believed that he was the fulfillment of that prophecy. Convinced that God would give his people the power to regain their freedom and rebuild the Temple, his revolt lasted from 132-35. His rebellion was supported by Rabbi Akiva, the most eminent legal authority of his day, who really believed that Simeon was the long-awaited Messiah. Interestingly, he accepted that the 10 northern tribes were really lost and did not expect his Messiah to gather them together again. The

Emperor Hadrian's program of Hellenization was the trigger for the revolution, which was initially very successful.

Simeon set up his own government; coins were minted in his name, and a nationwide system of deputies was introduced. In the end, however, the might of Rome was too strong. Reinforcements were sent in and, according to a later historian, hundreds of thousands of Jews were slaughtered in the ensuing battle during which the whole country was laid waste. By C.E. 135 the last rebel stronghold was under Roman control. The final defeat is said to have taken place on the ninth day of the month of Ab, which was also the anniversary of the destruction of both Solomon's Temple by the Babylonians, and of Herod's Temple by the Romans; it is still observed as a day of mourning in the Jewish community. Simeon himself was killed during the course of the campaign, while the learned and holy Rabbi Akiva was captured by the Romans and flayed alive. The Holy City of Jerusalem was closed to Jews, who were forbidden to live within its walls. A new Roman city, known as Aeolia Capitolina, was built on the site.

Meanwhile, many Jewish communities were thriving outside the Promised Land. After the death of Alexander the Great, his empire was divided between his generals. The Egyptian, Ptolemy, was tolerant of the Jewish religion, and many Jews were encouraged to move to the new city of Alexandria situated on the Nile delta. Here the community spoke Greek and within a few generations Hebrew was largely forgotten, and the Scriptures had to be translated. This translation is known as the Septuagint. It is so called because it is supposed to have been the work of 70 scholars. Its date is uncertain, but is generally reckoned as being 100 B.C.E. Because it is so early, the Scriptural Canon had not yet been settled and the order of the books is different from the order in the Hebrew Bible, and includes such works as Ecclesiasticus and Maccabees.

By the 1st century C.E., the Jews of Alexandria were largely self-governing and their central synagogue was famous for its splendor. The community was ruled over by an ethnarch and had its own court. There were Jewish poets, historians and dramatists. Most eminent of all was the philosopher Philo (c. 25 B.C.E.-40 B.C.E.), who interpreted the Scriptures in the light of Greek philosophy.

There was another large Jewish community in Rome. Jews were said to be conspicuous in their mourning for Julius Caesar in 44 B.C.E. and from the second half of the 1st century, the community was firmly established. There is archaeological evidence of no less than 12 synagogues, including one belonging to the Samaritans, and there are six Jewish catacombs yielding about 500 inscriptions.

Babylon was another important center of Jewish life. There had been a Jewish community in Babylon since the time of the Exile, and by the 2nd century C.E., the king of Persia, who ruled over Babylon, had formally recognized the leader of the Jewish community – the Exilarch. The Exilarchy was a hereditary office which, according to legend, dated back to King Jehoiachin, the last king of Judah descended from King David. He was responsible for the collection of taxes, for the appointment of judges, and for representing the Jews at the king's court. The Exilarch seems also to

Caesarea was the capital of the Roman Province of Judea. Named after Caesar Augustus, it has fine examples of aquaducts (RIGHT) and an impressive theatre (CENTRE RIGHT).

BELOW and FAR RIGHT: The ruins of the third century synagogue at Caperneum.

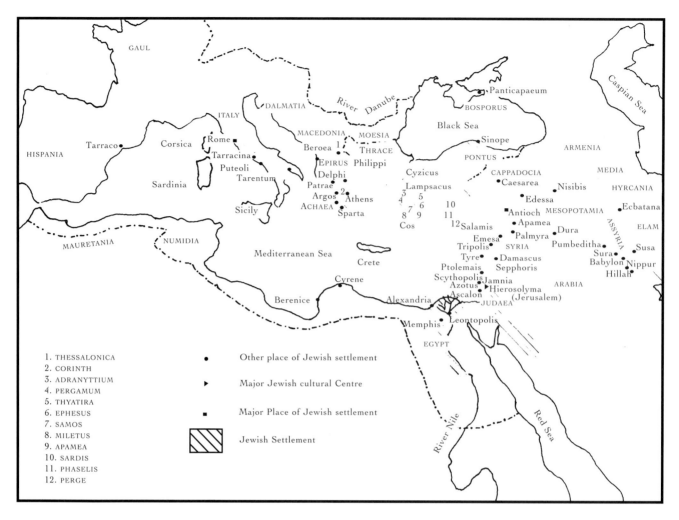

1. THESSALONICA
2. CORINTH
3. ADRANYTTIUM
4. PERGAMUM
5. THYATIRA
6. EPHESUS
7. SAMOS
8. MILETUS
9. APAMEA
10. SARDIS
11. PHASELIS
12. PERGE

●   Other place of Jewish settlement

▶   Major Jewish cultural Centre

■   Major Place of Jewish settlement

▨   Jewish Settlement

FAR LEFT: Map showing Jewish dispersion and settlement in Roman times.

LEFT: Remains of the synagogue at Kfar Biram, Galilee.

BELOW LEFT: An aerial view of Avdat, an important Nabatean town on the caravan route between Gaza and Petra.

have encouraged the emergence of an intelligentsia to oversee community administration which in turn supported the creation of the academies in the centers of Sura and Pumpedita where Jewish law was studied and discussed. These academies enjoyed enormous prestige in the Jewish world; their heads were known as *Geonim* (*Gaon* in the singular) and, in later years, there would be a tussle for power between the Exilarch and the Geonim.

Jews could be found in all the major cities of the Mediterranean. These communities did not always have an easy time: because of their religious practices, the Jews lived separately from their pagan neighbors and were frequently regarded with hostility. They did enjoy some privileges in the Roman Empire: because they were not prepared to march on the Sabbath, they were, for example, excused from service in the imperial army.

After the Jewish War of C.E. 70, many Jews outside Judaea rose in sympathy with their co-religionists in the Promised Land. There were notable rebellions in Alexandria, Cyrene and Cyprus, which were put down with utmost brutality. None-the-less, in general the Jews were tolerated. At this period it seems that Judaism was a missionary religion: in the New Testament, for instance, Jesus describes the Pharisees crossing "land and sea to make a single proselyte" (*St. Matthew*, Chapter 23.15.). The rabbis taught that converts to Judaism must be accorded exactly the same status as those who were born into the religion. The synagogues also seem to have attracted gentiles who were not willing to undergo the initiation rite of circumcision, but who were sympathetic to Jewish religious practice.

The Roman province of Judea was well populated and rich. Bet She'an provides a good example of a substantial Roman urban development. Among its architectural treasures is a remarkably well preserved Roman theatre which could seat 8,000.

They were known as "God-fearers" and are again mentioned in the New Testament. It is probable that many Jews today are ultimately descended from these people.

This settled state of affairs did not last, however. Once the Roman Emperor Constantine had adopted Christianity as the official religion of the empire in the 4th century, the position of Jews throughout the Mediterranean changed dramatically for the worse.

RIGHT: The streets of Subeita, dead city of the Negev

FAR RIGHT: The Tower of David Museum is an excellent place to view the history of Jerusalem.

CHAPTER FIVE

ORAL LAW

The Triumph of the Pharisees

Once the Temple had been destroyed in C.E. 70, there was no further role for the Sadducees. None-the-less, the hereditary principle survived: even today among the Jewish people, there are those who believe that they are descended from the priestly caste. Known as *Cohenim* [priests], they are still subject to certain ritual restrictions – for example, they may not marry a divorced woman or a convert to Judaism, and they are forbidden from coming into contact with the dead because this would lead to a state of ritual impurity. Their status entitles them to a certain degree of respect – traditionally they are the first to be called to read from the Torah scroll in the synagogue, and they have the right to pronounce a special priestly blessing. In fact, there is no way to be certain that those who believe themselves to be Cohanim are really descended from the Sadducees; it is merely a family legend, which has been handed down from generation to generation. Partly because of the dubiousness of the claim, modern Reform Judaism has dispensed with all the priestly regulations, and no longer recognizes the category. Among Orthodox Jews it persists.

With the Temple a charred ruin, it would have been easy for Judaism to disappear, as did so many of the cults of the ancient world. Its survival as a living religion is due to the vision of the Pharisaic leaders of the time. The story goes, that during the Roman siege of Jerusalem in C.E. 70, Rabban Johanan ben Zakkai managed to escape from the city with a group of disciples. He settled near the coast of the Mediterranean Sea in the town of Javneh, and gathered around him a group of scholars. Johanan was himself the grandson of the great Rabbi Hillel, who was the most eminent of all the sages of the second Temple period. Johanan carried on his grandfather's practice of discussing, interpreting, and explaining Jewish law. From far and wide, Pharisaic scholars joined the academy at Javneh; they learned from the masters and then, through the established network of synagogues, the legal conclusions were passed on to the people.

Johanan's successor was Rabban Gamaliel, who succeeded in re-establishing the supreme Jewish court, the Sanhedrin. In the court decisions seem to have been reached by majority vote after lengthy discussion. Students came from all over the Jewish world to listen to and learn from the debate, and the Sanhedrin was recognized, almost from its reinception, as the ultimate Jewish representative body both for the land of Israel, and for the Jewish populations of the Dispersion. It came to conclusions on such matters as the authorized Canon of Scripture, the organization of reg-

ular prayer, and the transfer of a modified form of Temple ritual to the synagogue. It regarded itself not only as the guarantor of the religious future, but also the guardian of the past. The teachings of the early Pharisees, such as Hillel and his great rival, Shammai, were rehearsed and summarized, and the details of Temple ritual were recalled and recited. The hope was maintained that one day the Temple would be restored again to all its former glory.

Perhaps most significant of all, a system of rabbinical ordination was introduced. The term *rabbi* simply means "my master," or "my teacher," and this mode of address was current even while the Temple was standing. It is

ABOVE: A modern rabbinical academy or Yeshivah in Jerusalem.

mentioned in the New Testament; on a couple of occasions, Jesus himself is called "rabbi" and, in turn, mocks those Pharisees who love "to be called by men rabbi." Later it became established that the title could only be given to those who had been properly ordained. Ordination was effected by the laying on of hands; this ceremony could only be performed in the Holy Land, and was accompanied by a special formula:

"May he teach? He may teach! May he give decisions? He may give decisions!"

All members of the Sanhedrin had undergone ordination, which gave their decisions particular weight.

Obviously, it was not possible for all scholars to make the long journey to the land of Israel. In Babylonia, in the academies, sages who were acknowledged as learned were described as "rav" rather than rabbi. In fact, even in the land of Israel, rabbinical ordination had ceased by the end of the 4th century. The term rabbi still continued to be used to describe legal authorities, however.

Different countries had different rabbinical customs. Sometimes a "Permission to teach" certificate was issued, which was signed by one or more eminent scholars. Later, oral examinations were introduced, which had to be passed before an individual could be recognized as being an authority in his own right. It must be pointed out that these early rabbis did not accept money for their services; even the most learned legal expert earned his living by some other means – for example by shoe-mending, tailoring or knife-grinding. It was only in the Middle Ages that the title of rabbi came to imply the spiritual leader of a particular community. In modern times, the congregational rabbi serves very much the same function as his Christian clerical counterpart: he runs the synagogue services, preaches regular sermons, visits the sick, celebrates life-cycle events, attends committee meetings, counsels the unhappy, raises funds and attends to the umpteen other matters which arise in a modern congregation. Despite this, the title does not describe a job, but denotes a qualification. It is quite possible for a rabbi to earn his living by, for example, selling life insurance, running a filling station or auditing industrial accounts, and still correctly use the title.

Despite Rabbi Akiva's involvement, the Bar Kokhba Revolt of 132 did not destroy the new structures. After this disaster, there were no further attempts at rebellion. The Jewish leaders pursued a policy of conciliation towards their Roman overlords, and the Sanhedrin flourished and provided a focus for Jewish religious life. New academies were founded, both in the land of Israel and Babylonia; new scholars came forward, listened to the debates, became experts themselves and received ordination or permission to teach. The legal interpretations were passed down from scholar to scholar through the generations and were disseminated to the people through countless village synagogues. Despite the catastrophic loss of the Temple and the humiliation of two crushed rebellions, the Jewish tradition not only survived, it developed and flourished.

BELOW: The Jewish World in C. E. 300

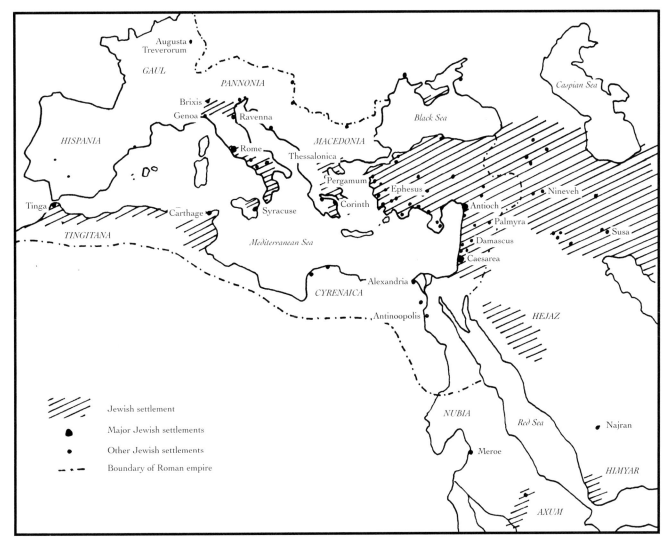

The priests, their heads covered with prayer shawls recite the Priestly Blessing at the Western Wall.

The Tannaim and the Mishnah

With the re-establishment of the Sanhedrin, a Jewish hierarchy was recognized in Israel. The head of the Sanhedrin was known as the *Nasi* [Prince]; Rabban Gamaliel II was acknowledged as the first, and, once peace had been established with the Romans, he was entrusted with the collection of taxes, the appointment of judges for the community, and the maintenance of contact with coreligionists in the Dispersion. Under the new structure, there was a renewal of Jewish scholarship, and among the distinguished rabbis of the late 1st century were Eliezar ben Hyrcanus, Joshua ben Hanina, Tarphon and Ishmael ben Elijah. Rabbi Akiva was the giant of the next generation, while late-2nd-century authorities included Simeon ben Gamaliel II, Simeon bar Yohai, and Meir. There was a strong sense of continuity from the very earliest times. According to the *Sayings of the Fathers*, which was compiled in the 3rd century:

"Moses received the Law from Sinai and handed it down to Joshua, and Joshua to the Elders, and the Elders to the Prophets and the Prophets handed it down to the Men of the Great Assembly . . . Simon the Just was one of the last survivors of the Great Assembly . . . Antigonus of Seho received the tradition from Simon the Just . . . José ben Joezar and José ben Johanan received it from them . . . Joshua ben Perahiah and Nittai the Arbelite received it from them . . . Judah ben Tabbai and Simon ben Shetah received it from them . . . Shemaiah and Abtalion received it from them . . . Hillel and Shammai received it from them."

The chain survived despite the destruction of the Temple. Johanan ben Zakkai was the grandson of Hillel; his successor was Rabban Gamaliel II. Gamaliel's son, Simon, was another eminent legal authority, who is credited with the sayings, "By three things is the world preserved: by truth, by judgment and by peace" and, "All my days I have grown up among the Wise, and I have found nothing of better service than silence; not learning, but doing is the chief thing; and who is profuse of words causes sin" (*Sayings of the Fathers*, Chapter 1). The son of Simon ben Gamaliel II was Judah ha-Nasi.

By the start of the 3rd century, the oral interpretation of the Law had become highly complex. There had been earlier attempts at its codification, notably by Akiva and Meir, but something more comprehensive had become necessary. What was needed was an authoritative record of the debates and decisions of all these scholars, or *tannaim*, as they were called. Judah ha-Nasi set himself the task of making a compilation; the final result is the *Mishnah* (oral law).

It is an extraordinary document. Nearly 150 tannaim are mentioned by name. The actual opinions given are recorded with the minority view expressed first, and the final decision set down at the end. The usual formula is "Rabbi Joshua says . . . but the Sages declare that . . ." The whole is divided into six orders, according to subject matter: "Seeds," which lists the laws of agriculture, "Fixed Seasons" on the laws of fasts, festivals and

the Sabbath, "Women," which contains the laws of marriage and divorce, "Damages," on civil and criminal law, "Holy Matters," which discusses sacrifice and Temple ritual and "Cleanliness," which covers the complex matter of ritual purity. Thus the Mishnah provides a full guide to everyday Jewish living, as well as a definitive record of the practices of the priests in the Temple.

ABOVE: Rabbi Meir's Tomb, Tiberias

In addition, in the order of "Damages," it contains one of the best-loved books in Jewish literature, the *Sayings of the Fathers*. This is an anthology of rabbinical maxims and moral saws. Nowadays it is printed in most editions of the Jewish prayer book, and it is a treasure trove of wisdom:

"Hillel said: Do not separate yourself from the congregation; do not trust in yourself until the day of your death . . . Do not say: When I have leisure, I will study; perhaps you will never have leisure . . ."

"Rabbi Ishmael said: Be submissive to a superior, affable to a suppliant and receive all men with cheerfulness."

"Rabbi Akiva said: Everything is foreseen, yet freedom of choice is given."

"Great is the Torah which gives life to those that practise it in this world . . . It is a tree of life to them that grasp it and of them that uphold it, everyone is made happy."

The Mishnah does not include all the existing oral law. A parallel collection, known as the *Tosefta* [supplement] also survives. It too is divided into six orders, with the same titles as those of the Mishnah. The importance of these collections is that they provided a solid base line upon which further discussion and interpretation could take place.

The tannaim were also concerned with explaining and interpreting the text of the Hebrew scriptures. (Rabbinical interpretation of the Bible is known as *midrash*.) Before the destruction of the Temple, Rabbi Hillel had laid down seven fundamental rules of exegesis; in the 2nd century, Rabbi Ishmael expanded these rules to 13. They are complicated, enable apparent contradictions within the text to be reconciled, and encourage inference from one passage to another. Direct exegeis was also encouraged so that a scholar might expound a text according to its plain meaning. For example, *Deuteronomy* 15.11 "You shall open wide your hand to your brother" is explained by saying that it is your duty to fulfill your brother's particular needs: "To him for whom bread is suitable, give bread; to him for whom dough is suitable give dough; to him for whom money is required, give money."

The tannaim were convinced that by diligently studying the Scriptures and the Law, God's will would continue to be revealed to his chosen people. The Temple lay in ruins but the word of the Lord survived and continued to inspire the Jewish nation.

The Amoraim and the Talmud

The amoraim were the successors of the tannaim. By the end of the 4th century, oral law in the land of Israel had developed still further. Using Judah ha-Nasi's Mishnah as the basis for discussion, additional material, known as the *Gemara,* was collected and put together. Four of the six orders of the Mishnah have Gemara; it may be that there were also interpretations of "Holy Matters" and "Cleanliness" which are now lost. Most scholars believe that the Gemara on "Damages" was compiled earlier than that of the other three orders. Collectively, this work, the whole Mishnah and the Gemara on the four orders, is known as the *Palestinian Talmud*. It is written in the Western Aramaic dialect, and it seems to have been the work of scholars from the three academies of Caesarea, Tiberias and Sepphoris. It has many internal contradictions and there is little attempt to edit out the repetitions.

Similar activity was taking place in the academies of Babylon. Rav Ashi, of the academy at Sura, is reputed to have started the process of compilation, and the final text of what became known as the *Babylonian Talmud* was completed in the 6th century. It is a huge work: although it covers slightly fewer tractates than its Palestinian counterpart, it is almost four times as long. Both works record the give-and-take of the debate. In the Mishnah a principle is generally the starting point, but the discussion ranges over many subjects. The Talmud has been compared with the sea: there is no attempt at systematizing the argument, which includes nonlegal material, theology, folklore, legends, jokes, magical spells and ethical saws. Material is not presented in a logical manner; as in any conversation or debate, the speakers go off at a tangent, introducing irrelevances and often skipping stages in the argument. It is not easy to find one's way about, for example, if one should want to know the laws for writing a Torah scroll, they are to be found in the tractate on meal offerings in the Temple. The regulations for the festival of Hanukkah are to be located in a tractate on the Sabbath.

RIGHT: The so-called Tower of David in Jerusalem — now a museum.

The *Babylonian Talmud* is largely written in the eastern Aramaic dialect, and it reflects the daily life of the Jewish people in the 5th and 6th centuries C.E. It provides laws for the guidance and good order of the community; it also gives us information on contemporary ideas on history, astronomy, zoology, botany, agriculture and medicine. Customs and superstitions are included, as are popular proverbs, fairy tales, prayers, rules of manners, parables and reminders of the laws of etiquette. The wisdom of the simple is recorded, as well as the pronouncements of the sages. It is really one long, free association of ideas.

It must be remembered that the *Babylonian Talmud* was produced long before the days of printing; copies had to be made by hand and then painstakingly recopied. Inevitably, errors crept in, and there are innumerable variant readings of the text. None-the-less, from the moment it was written down, the Talmud was regarded as an authoritative work. Although there were two Talmuds, the Palestinian and the Babylonian, the Babylonian is regarded as being the most important. There is a Jewish legal principle that maintains that the final decision accords with the view of the later authority. The *Palestinian Talmud* was compiled 150 years before the Babylonian, so when there is a contradiction, the Babylonian version is to be preferred.

Increasingly during this period, the Babylonian community was eclipsing the Palestinian and the academies of Sura and Pumbedita had become the most important centers in world Jewry. As we will see later in this chapter, Jewish communities tended to be better treated under Islamic than under Christian rule. The Exilarch and the Geonim (the heads of the academies) were regarded as the leaders of the Jewish world by the Muslim rulers. Thus the importance of the *Babylonian Talmud* cannot be exaggerated in the history of the Jewish people. It has been a source of knowledge, and inspiration, a community treasure and, in many cases, has formed the entire curriculum in Jewish schools.

Even today, the Talmud is the major set text in *yeshivot* (Jewish academies). In addition to their secular education, strictly Orthodox young men are still expected to spend several years studying in a yeshiva. Here they all work together in one big room (the *Bet Ha-Midrash* – house of study). Generally reading in tandem with another boy, a study-partner of similar ability, the scholar will make his painstaking way through page after page of the Talmud. The Talmud is generally printed in a particular format in which the essential passage of the Mishnah is set in the middle of the page followed by the relevant (longer) Gemara passage. Then, surrounding this essential core, are further explanations of the text written by later eminent authorities. It is an extraordinary mental training and there are many delightful stories about life in a yeshiva. *Yentl the Yeshiva Boy*, by Sholom Aleichem, gives much of the flavor of Talmudic study in 19th-century Eastern Europe, and is well-known through the musical movie *Yentl*.

An example of yeshiva life follows: it is said that a Master caught two boys gazing at a bird out of the window when they should have been studying the text. "What does the bird make you think of?" the Master asked. One boy replied, "The bird makes me think of the soul soaring to heaven."

"Nonsense!" said the Master, "Concentrate on your work!" The other boy said, "Well Master, when I saw that bird, I started wondering what would happen if it suddenly dropped down dead and fell on the boundary fence of two neighbors. I was trying to work out how you would decide to which neighbor the corpse of the bird would belong." "Ah," said the Master, "Here is someone who understands the point of Talmud study!"

Further Dispersion

In the 4th century Christianity became the official religion of the Roman Empire and Jews quickly became subject to various legal restrictions. Jews who converted their Christian wives were liable to the death penalty, while marriage between a Christian and a Jew was declared to be adulterous. By the 5th century, Jews were forbidden positions in the civil service or in the army; Jewish courts were only permitted to judge private cases between Jews; and synagogues could only be repaired with special permission.

There was enormous pressure for Jews to convert to Christianity, and there is no doubt that many succumbed. By the early 7th century, the baptism of all Jews was demanded in Byzantium, France and Spain. In fact, this was not enforced, and the Christian kings often found it advantageous to have some Jews within their kingdoms, for the Jews had international connections which were useful in establishing trade, and since Jews were increasingly forbidden to own land, they turned to moneylending as a means of making a living. Throughout the Middle Ages, the Christian church was unequivocal in its condemnation of lending money upon interest. Because there was no gain in it for them, Christians were therefore unwilling to lend money; Jewish law does not allow charging interest to fellow Jews, but it is permitted to outsiders. Thus, in addition to their trading contacts, the Jews were a constant source of loans – hence the stereotype of the avaricious Jewish usurer that we find in Shakespeare's *Merchant of Venice* and Marlowe's *Jew of Malta*.

Meanwhile, another power was rising in the East. In the 7th century, the Arab peoples of the Arabian Peninsula were polytheists; they either lived in towns or, as nomads, wandered from place to place. The prophet Muhammad denounced the paganism of his countrymen, and claimed that he had received a divine revelation of Allah, the One True God. This superseded the revelation given to Abraham, Moses and Jesus, and was written down in the *Koran*, the ultimate word of God. Initially, Muhammad had hoped to convert the Jews of the peninsula to his way of thinking, but the community rejected his message. Consequently, he denounced the Jews as infidels and insisted that they had distorted the message of Allah. He accepted that the Torah was divinely inspired, but he insisted that it needed the Koran to correct and fulfill it.

The progress of Islam was astonishing: by C.E. 644 Syria, Israel, Egypt, Iraq and Persia had become part of the new Islamic Empire. By the start of the 8th century, Muslim soldiers had crossed North Africa, had reached the Straits of Gibraltar and were bent on conquering Spain. Initially, this did not seem to be good news for the Jews: following Muhammad's orders, by

626 two Jewish tribes had been expelled from the city of Medina, and a third had been exterminated. None-the-less, Jews normally did well under Muslim rule. In the Islamic Empire both Christians and Jews were recognized as being "People of the Book." Provided they accepted the supremacy of the Muslim state, they were guaranteed exemption from military service and were granted religious autonomy and toleration.

With the conquest of Babylonia, the Muslim caliph formally acknowledged the role of the Exilarch as the head of the Dispersion Jewish community. He represented his people at court and shared his power with the Geonim, the heads of the academies. The political stability of the Islamic Empire enabled religious networks to be established, and the Geonim invited questions about Jewish law from the communities of the Dispersion, and would send back their *Responsa* [answers]. The free movement of peoples enabled Jews to establish new centers, and they even carried on trade beyond the empire's boundaries. According to legend, in the 9th century, Jewish merchants converted the king of the Khazar tribe (a group who lived on the Volga River) to Judaism.

RIGHT: During the fourth century a Byzantine monastery was built on the Mount of Temptation on the site of an Herodian fort. This is Mar Saba near Jericho.

Jewish liberties within the empire were guaranteed by the Pact of Omar, according to which the Jews could not make converts: had to pay an additional poll tax; and had to wear distinctive clothing. Apart from this they were permitted to live in peace, free from the fear of persecution. As a result new academies were established; very prominent from the 10th century were the academies of Israel, particularly at Tiberias and Rameleh, and of North Africa. There were centers of Jewish learning in Cairo in Egypt, Kairouan in Tunisia and Fez in Morocco. Meanwhile, the academies of Sura and Pumbedita had moved to Baghdad, the seat of the caliphate. Perhaps the greatest blossoming of Jewish culture was in southern Spain, where the works of such poets as Judah Halevy, Moses ibn Ezra and Solomon ibn Gabirol were written and subsequently enshrined in the Jewish liturgy even to this day. There were also several prominent Jewish statesmen, such as Hasdai ibn Shaprut in the 10th century and Samuel ha-Nagid in the 11th century. Talmudic, philosophical and mystical learning also flourished.

Meanwhile, things were less happy in Christian Europe. The Christian authorities did not recognize a single Jewish Exilarch, so different communities established different customs; some were highly successful. There were important centers of Jewish learning in northern France and in the Rhineland. The great biblical commentator Rashi and his school, the Tosafists, produced commentaries on all the books of the Bible and the orders of the Talmud.

The Arab and Muslim expansion of the seventh century soon wrested the Holy Land from the Byzantines and set the stage for centuries of warfare with Christendom. One of the oldest — and certainly the most holy — Muslim sites in the Middle East is the Dome of the Rock (RIGHT), built to protect the rock on which Abraham was preparing to sacrifice his son Isaac. It was built in 691 C.E.

ABOVE: Another, later, example of Muslim architecture — the White Tower of Ramle.

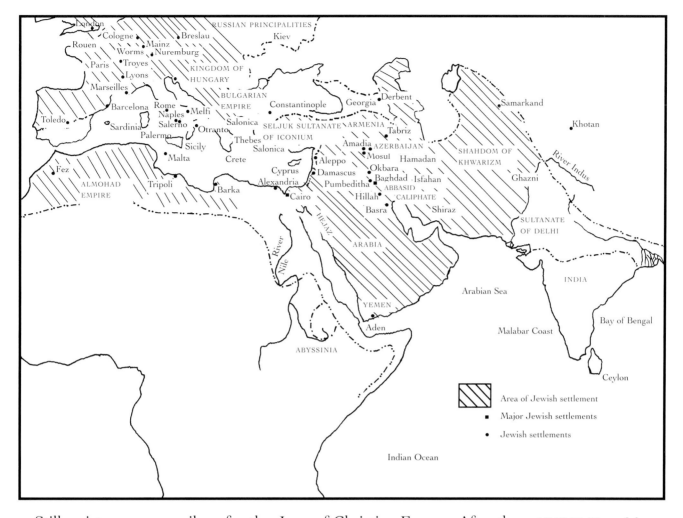

Still, existence was perilous for the Jews of Christian Europe. After the First Crusade at the end of the 11th century, Jews were massacred in several Rhineland towns. By the middle of the 12th century, the first blood libel was recorded: Jews were accused of using the blood of Christian children in the manufacture of unleavened bread. Debates and disputations between Jewish scholars and members of the Dominican order were conducted, after which the Talmud was publicly condemned and burned. Also, as the Christian kings made use of Jewish moneylenders and their debts correspondingly piled up, they began to see the expulsion of the Jews as the solution to their economic difficulties. In 1290 the Jews were expelled from England, and the French king followed the English example a few years later.

In the next century, when the Black Death raged throughout Europe, the Jews were widely blamed for the plague: they were said to have poisoned the wells. In the 14th and 15th centuries, massacre and expulsion became a frequent part of the Jewish experience. The great exception was Poland, where Jews were protected from the 13th century onward: here Jews became tax collectors, fiscal agents and the managers of great noblemen's estates. But there was no such security elsewhere in Catholic Europe: Spain had been reconquered by those most Christian of monarchs, Ferdinand and Isabella, and by their orders in 1492 all Jews were expelled from Spanish soil. The great Jewish community of the Iberian Peninsula was thus scattered to North Africa, Turkey, the Low Countries and Italy.

ABOVE: Map of the Jewish World in 1200

The Karaites

The rabbis claimed that the oral law as found in the Talmud had originally been communicated by God to Moses on Mount Sinai at the same time as the written law. As Rabbi Simon ben Lakish put it,

"The Lord said to Moses: Come up to me to the mountain and I will give you the stone tablets and the Torah and the Commandment which I have inscribed to instruct them' (*Exodus* 24.12), should be understood as follows: 'the stone tablets' refer to the Ten Commandments; 'and the Torah' refers to the Pentateuch; 'and the Commandment' refers to the Mishnah; 'which I have inscribed' refers to the prophets and the writings; 'to instruct them' refers to the Gemara – and all this teaching was given to Moses on Mount Sinai."

As we have already seen, this was not a universal opinion. While the Temple was still standing, the Sadducees, the aristocratic, priestly caste, only accepted the authority of the written law. It was the Pharisees, the middle-class scribes and students of the law who preached in the synagogue, who insisted that the oral law was of equal value. After the destruction of the Temple in C.E. 70, there was no further role for the Sadducees, and the Pharisaic view prevailed. The Jewish world increasingly centered

An overview of the
Karaite settlement

ABOVE: The walls of the Old City of Jerusalem were built in the 16th century by Suleiman the Magnificent.

RIGHT: The Crusader castle of Belvoir was built high above the Jordan valley, one of many such strategic strongholds the Christian knights erected in their wars with the Arabs.

around the academies of Babylonia and Israel where the Law was studied, discussed and interpreted, and from where authoritative *Responsa* (replies) to the legal queries of the far-flung Dispersion communities were issued.

Yet scepticism in some quarters toward the oral law remained. In the 9th century, a threat to the unity of the Jewish world was posed by the emergence of an anti-rabbinic sect. The problem had begun in the 760s, when one Anan ben David had been passed over for the Exilarchy in favor of his younger brother. According to the story, Anan, in fury, set himself up as a rival Exilarch. Initially he was imprisoned by the caliph, but Anan claimed to be the head of a different religion and was accordingly given the benefit of Muslim religious tolerance. The historical tradition about Anan is unreliable, but he is credited with being the founder of what came to be called Karaism.

The Karaites themselves trace their origin to the split between the northern and southern kingdom after the death of King Solomon in the 10th century B.C.E. They believe that Zadok, Solomon's high priest, had preserved the truth and had handed it down through his descendants the Sadducees (the name Sadducee may well be derived from that of Zadok). Anan's fundamental principle was said to be "Search thoroughly in the Torah and do not rely on my opinion." He was convinced that the will of God could be found in its entirety in the Pentateuch and that there was no need for the rabbis oral interpretations. Anan insisted that Jewish practice must accord not with rabbinical ordinances, but with biblical legislation.

The fact that the Karaites rejected rabbinism did not make the yoke of the law any easier, for in some ways the Karaite leaders interpreted the legal tradition more severely. For example, they were even more stringent in their definition of forbidden Sabbath work; the circumcision ceremony was subject to even more complex regulations; there were more days of fasting; ritual cleanliness was taken very seriously indeed; and the minimal quantities of forbidden foods accepted by the rabbis were rejected. In addition, many Islamic traditions were adopted: Karaite synagogues did not have chairs; shoes were removed on entry, and worshippers knelt and prostrated themselves during prayer.

After Anan's death there was no clear leader of the movement, and it seems to have split into innumerable small groups and sects. The strict followers of Anan called themselves Ananites, and lived mainly in Egypt. Other groups were more liberal in their approach: they were criticized by the rabbis for having too many diverse opinions, but, as one early leader put it, "The Rabbis believe that their laws and regulations were transmitted by the prophets; if that were the case, there ought not to exist any difference of opinion amongst them . . . We, on the other hand, arrive at our views by our reason, and reason can lead to various results." By the 9th century, a consensus had emerged, and by the 10th century there were successful Karaite communities in North Africa, Egypt, Persia, Babylonia and Israel. There was a conscious attempt to spread Karaite doctrines through the Jewish community, but this was resisted by staunch rabbinites such as the learned Saadiah Gaon.

The land of Israel was the center for Karaite scholarship until the late

11th century, where Karaite scholars produced some outstanding biblical translations and exegeses. Many of the later Masoretes, who set out the rules regarding the correct spelling, writing and reading of the Bible, may have had Karaite sympathies. Both the rabbinite and Karaite communities of Israel were destroyed in the Crusades, but later Karaite communities were founded in the Byzantine Empire, in the Crimea and in Poland and Lithuania, and in general, Karaites were regarded as Jews by their host nations. Ultimately however, the intellectual tide turned against them, and by the late 16th century, Karaism was in decline.

Yet there are still Karaites in the world today: the small communities in Eastern Europe were spared by the Nazis on the grounds that they were not of Jewish stock. The founding fathers of the state of Israel knew better, and when there were signs of persecution in the Arab countries, Karaites were invited to settle in Israel under the Law of Return. Today it is thought that there are about 7,000 Karaites in Israel, a few thousand in Russia (with which contact was cut off during the communist years), about 1,500 in California, perhaps a hundred families in Istanbul and a tiny group in Cairo. Their spiritual leader has been designated the Chief Rabbi of the Karaite Jews in Israel. There still are some problems, however: because of slightly different laws of marriage and divorce, both the Karaites and the rabbinites suspect each others' legitimacy, and there are strong community objections to intermarriage. None-the-less, as with the Samaritans, there is every reason to hope that this interesting sect will continue to survive into the 3rd millennium in the Jewish state.

CHAPTER SIX

PHILOSOPHERS AND MYSTICS

*The Early
Medieval
Philosophers*

The Mishnah and Talmud are not works of philosophy, but behind the legends, parables and moral maxims contained in them, a clear rabbinical world view emerges. God is One; this is the daily declaration of every pious Jew. He is the sole creator, the only source of the universe and the one guide of providence. Idolatry is to be condemned absolutely. God is the transcendent origin of everything that is; at the same time, He is immanent and intimately concerned with the affairs of His world. As the rabbis put it, "He is as near to His creatures as the ear is near to the mouth." The people of Israel have a special place in God's scheme of things: He liberated them from slavery in Egypt for a purpose, so that they would receive the yoke of the Commandments and bring the knowledge of God to the world. Thus the study of God's word in His Torah and Talmud is the ultimate duty for every Jew. Every word, every letter, is sacred and through its wisdom, God Himself is to be found.

In the first century C.E., the Alexandrian philosopher Philo attempted to interpret Jewish thought in the light of Greek philosophy. He himself had been influenced by the Stoic school, and he explained the Scriptures using an allegorical method. Later Jewish philosophers also tried to reconcile fundamental Jewish concepts with the philosophical ideas of their times. In the early Middle Ages, for example, they were particularly influenced by the Islamic Kalam schools. Through the medium of the Arab language, Jews came into contact with Muslim theology and, through it, to Greek philosophy. (The Muslims, of course, insisted that God's revelation to Moses had been superseded by the word of God as recorded in Muhammad's Koran.) Meanwhile, within the Jewish ranks, the Karaites were arguing that the rabbinical view of God was nonbiblical and frequently anthropomorphic. Then the Zoroastrians and Manicheans were maintaining that the idea of the one god could not be the foundation of a reliable religious system since it failed to take account of the reality and origin of evil.

Between the 9th and the 14th centuries, philosophy became a central focus for concern for many in the Jewish community. The great Jewish philosopher of the 10th century, Saadiah ben Joseph al Fayyumi (882-942), known as Saadiah Gaon, attempted to counter the teachings of the Muslims, Zoroastrians and those who believed that the existence of the universe required no divine explanation at all. Saadiah's *Emunot ve Deot* (Book of Beliefs and Opinions) is generally regarded as the first Jewish philosophical classic. In it, he insisted that there was no conflict between the findings of reason and the discoveries of revealed religion. He taught that the universe could not always have been there, and that the Creator called the world into being out of nothing. Despite God's many attributes. He is One, not a plurality. Saadiah responded to the Karaite accusation of anthropomorphism by pointing out that the inadequacy of human language compels us to speak of God in human terms, but that these descriptions were never intended to be taken literally. Then, against the Muslims, he maintained that the written and oral Jewish law was valid for all time. God's Commandments were given in order to create a successful communal life, and to promote individual self-discipline. He believed that it was in the afterlife that God would reward the faithful and punish the wicked.

Saadiah influenced the generations of Jewish philosophers who came after him. In the 11th century, many Muslim thinkers had returned to fundamentalist values and were increasingly denying that logical thinking and the evidence of the senses were the sources of reliable knowledge and instead insisted on an unquestioning acceptance of the teachings of the Koran. Jewish philosophers therefore ceased to look to the Muslim tradition for inspiration, but turned to the Neoplatonic and Aristotelian systems of thought. Solomon ben Joseph ibn Gabirol (*c.* 1022-70) produced one of the earliest works in the Neoplatonic tradition. His *Fons Vitae* (Fountain of Life – it only survives in a Latin translation) argued that human beings are microcosms not only of the material, but also of the intelligible world. He taught that our physical universe issued forth from God, the spiritual Creator, at the end of a long chain of emanations. He believed that the world consists of cosmic existences, all flowing from the light of God and reflecting His glory. The idea of emanation was to become very influential on the thinking of the later Jewish mystics.

Another important philosophical work of the period was *Emunah Ramah* (The Exalted Faith), written by Abraham ben David Halevi ibn Daud (*c.* 1110-80). It was strongly influenced by the thought of the Greek philosopher, Aristotle, and it argued that God's Oneness, His absolute unity, could be deduced from His necessary existence. Ibn Daud insisted that the ultimate duty of human beings was to achieve perfect knowledge, and that this could be identified with the acquisition of faith. Earlier, Joseph ibn Pakuda (*c.* 1050-1120), in his *Hovot Ha-Levavot* (Duties of the Heart), had maintained that the human soul is of divine origin, and that through various spiritual steps the reader could reach communion with God and hence ultimate perfection.

Perhaps the best-known Jewish philosopher of this early medieval period was Judah Halevi (1075-1141). His *Kuzari* (Book of the Khazars) draws on the legend of the conversion of the Khazar tribe to Judaism. In the book, the Khazar king is shown listening to a defense of Judaism against the teachings of Islam, Christianity and Aristotelianism. In insisting that divine revelation rather than rational thought was the ultimate source of religious belief, Halevi offered an important challenge to the Aristotelian rationalism that was so fashionable in the early 12th century.

Views of Jerusalem. Following the dispersal of the Jews it would not be until the 20th century that "Next year in Jerusalem" became more a real possibility than a wish.

Maimonides

Probably the leading intellectual figure of medieval Jewry was Rabbi Moses ben Maimon (1135-1204), known as Maimonides, or RaMBaM. Not only was he a major philosopher, but he also contributed to the Jewish legal tradition. He produced an extraordinary synthesis of Jewish law known as the *Mishneh Torah* (the Second Law). It is the first of the great legal codes, is organized within a logical framework and it enabled the great legal tradition of the Jews to be studied by people who had neither the time nor the learning to study the Talmud. It is comprehensive in scope and covers the whole compass of Jewish law, even in areas no longer operative, such as those dealing with the ritual of the Temple.

The Mishneh Torah includes a discussion on the fundamentals of the Jewish faith; such subjects as the divine attributes of God, His nature, and the function of religious language are covered. However Maimonides's major philosophical work was the *Dalilat al-Hariain* (in Hebrew, *Moreh Nevukhim*, the Guide to the Perplexed). It was originally written in Arabic for the secular Jews at the time and was an attempt to reconcile the principles of Aristotelian philosophy with the traditional teachings of the rabbis.

Maimonides himself had a turbulent life. He was born in Cordoba in Spain. At that period the Almohads, a fanatical Moroccan dynasty, had conquered Spain, and the old tradition of religious tolerance disappeared. Jews were forced to convert to Islam, and synagogues and Talmudic academies were closed down. In common with many of his fellow-countrymen, Maimonides fled to North Africa. He became head of the Jewish community of Fostat in 1175 and, by profession a physician, was appointed court physician to Saladin's grand vizier in 1185. Thus he was well-acquainted with the non-Jewish world, and was in an admirable position to understand the perplexities of his highly assimilated coreligionists.

Maimonides argued that the anthropomorphic language used to describe God in the Hebrew Scriptures must be understood metaphorically. He discussed the various philosophical proofs for the existence of God, the nature of good and evil, the doctrine of divine providence, the position of Moses, and the nature and purpose of the Commandments. Behind his formidable intelligence and learning lay a devout faith; as he himself put it:

"Let not the wise man glory in his wisdom, let not the mighty man glory in his might, let not the rich man glory in his riches, but let him who glories glory in this, that he understands and knows the Lord who practices steadfast love, justice and righteousness in the earth."

His philosophy was extraordinarily influential, and was known by such Christian writers as Albertas Magnus and Thomas Aquinas. Within the Jewish community, it was the source of considerable controversy. On the one hand, the highly cultured and largely secular members of the upper stratum of society welcomed the attempt to synthesize rabbinical learning with classical philosophy. The Spanish scholar Nahmanides (1197-1270) defended the *Dalilat al-Hariain* on the grounds that Spanish Jewry was so assimilated that, without the writings of Maimonides, it would have been lost altogether to Judaism. On the other hand, the pious commentators and legal experts of northern France were appalled and anathematized Maimonides and his work in a flurry of letters and visits, sermons and warnings, accusations and counteraccusations. The community was, however, taken aback when members of the Christian Dominican order publicly burned the philosopher's books in 1232, and when his tomb in Tiberias was subsequently desecrated.

None-the-less, the conflict between the rationalists and the counter-rationalists rumbled on within the community – indeed, even before the time of Maimonides, Judah Halevi, the author of the *Kuzari* had warned: "Let not Greek wisdom tempt you, for it bears flowers only and no fruit." At the end of the 13th century, Solomon ben Abraham Adret of Barcelona went so far as to insist that Greek metaphysics should only be studied by mature men over the age of 25, but this was opposed by other Spanish and Provençal authorities.

This ambivalent attitude toward philosophy was also reflected in the response to the work of another prominent Jewish scholar after Maimonides, Levi ben Gershom, known as Gersonides (1288-1344), whose most important philosophical work was *Milhamot Adonai* (Wars of the Lord). He was also deeply influenced by the ideas of Aristotle, but went further in this than Maimonides. For example, he maintained that the universe was formed out of pre-existent eternal matter and not out of nothing, and he taught that God's providence was concerned with universals and not with the individual fate of human beings. He also discussed such matters as miracles, the nature of the soul, and the phenomenon of prophecy. Gersonides was sharply criticized by his successors, and is generally regarded as being the last of the Jewish Aristotelian philosophers.

Later Jewish thinkers deliberately distanced themselves from the ideas of Maimonides. Hasdai Crescas (1340-1412) of Barcelona denied the traditional proofs for the existence of God, and insisted that the only certain base was the authority of the Scriptures, the revealed word of God. Maimonides had outlined 13 fundamental principles of the Jewish faith, but these were criticized by Crescas. Isaac Abravanel (1437-1508) felt that the whole attempt to isolate fundamental principles was mistaken, since the whole Torah was equally divinely inspired and thus of equal value.

By the end of the 15th century, the use of Greek philosophy to defend the Jewish religion from rational assault had largely been abandoned. Later in the 17th century, the great Dutch figure, Baruch Spinoza, became deeply influenced by the work of Descartes; he was completely rejected by the Jewish community of his day, however, and his place is in the general history of Western thought rather than in Jewish philosophy. The Jewish people instead increasingly turned their attention to the mystical tradition as a basis of speculation about God and creation and the works of the secular philosophers, the Stoics, the Kalam school, the Neoplatonists and the Aristotelians, were deemed to be un-Jewish and dangerous to the faith of Abraham, Moses and the prophets.

The Early Medieval Mystics

In the early rabbinical literature and in the great morass of the Talmud there are hints of mystical speculation. Yet it was always the tradition that such speculation should, in some way, remain secret. There is a story about the early rabbis Simeon ben Jehozadak and Samuel ben Nahum. When Simeon asked how light was created, Samuel answered his question in a whisper. He explained: "Just as I myself had it whispered to me, even so have I whispered it to you." It was always said that mystical knowledge should only be given to a man who was pious and gentle, of middle age, calm, moderate in his habits and not inclined to vengeful feelings.

Within this early tradition, various elements can be distinguished. First of all there is chariot mysticism: this is based on the first chapter of the biblical book of Ezekiel where God's chariot is described in detail. The aim of chariot mysticism was to become a chariot rider, for it was thought possible to free oneself from one's physical chains and ascend in the chariot to the heavenly heights. Some particularly holy people were believed to have done so, and to have returned to tell the tale. Their stories are recorded in the so-called "heavenly hall" literature which dates from the 7th to 9th centuries.

During the same period there was a great deal of speculation about the whole process of creation. It was believed that the early chapters of the Book of Genesis had deeper esoteric meanings than it first appeared. The most famous early work dealing with this subject was the *Sefer Yetzirah* (Book of Creation), which taught that the entire universe was created from 32 paths made up from 10 emanations of God, and the 22 letters of the Hebrew alphabet.

The letters were thought to have particular meanings: three stood for the elements – air, fire and water – and the corresponding organs in human beings: the brain, the heart, and the stomach. Seven letters stood for the seven stars in the sky, the seven days of the week, and the seven orifices of the human senses. The 12 final letters corresponded to the 12 signs of the zodiac, the 12 months of the year, the 12 limbs of the body, and the 12 chief human activities. Human beings were thus seen as microcosms of the whole of the creation, and within this system everything in the universe was thought to have been composed from a combination of the letters.

Of the 10 emanations of God, the first was His Spirit. The second was air, which is derived from God's Spirit, and from which the Hebrew letters were thought to be hewn. Water was the third, from which was derived the chaos and darkness with which God created the universe. This was followed by fire, from which God formed the angles of heaven and the divine, fiery chariot. The final six emanations were the six spatial dimensions: north, south, east, west, height and depth. The early mystics taught that since everything comes into existence through God's emanations, God is emanant in the world. He Himself, however, is completely transcendent and apart from His creation.

The *Sefer Yetzirah* was particularly studied by the German Jews in the early Middle Ages. It was a troubled time in Christian Europe: the forces of Christendom were attempting to drive the Muslims from the Holy Land in the Crusades; rumors were circulating that a "Prince of Babylon" had destroyed the Holy Sepulcher in Jerusalem. Massacres of Jews became commonplace; the first took place in Speyer in 1096, another in Worms, and a third in Mainz. The slaughter was terrible, even though some bishops and noblemen tried to save the Jews under their protection. In 1146 there was another anti-Semitic outburst during the preaching of another crusade by Pope Eugenius III and St. Bernard of Clairvaux. The Third Crusade led to still more persecution of Jews.

The renewal of interest in mysticism must be understood against this background. There were several groups of scholars who flourished independently of each other during this period; collectively they are known as the *Hasidei Ashkenaz* (the pious men of Germany). Prominent among them was Rabbi Judah ben Samuel he-Hasid, who was the author of the *Sefer Hasidim* (Book of the Pious). This was a detailed exposition of ethics which discussed such subjects as prayer, worship, study, education, social and family relationships and dealings with non-Jews. Rabbi Judah put particular emphasis on effort and sacrifice. The more effort a righteous deed requires, then the more meritorious it is. Sin can only be atoned for by self-afflicted suffering, and martyrdom for the Jewish faith is to be seen as the ultimate good deed. Through this teaching, Judah prepared his community for the trials of Christian anti-Semitism. He gave them a theology which would sustain them through this difficult period.

Other important members of the *Hasidei Ashkenaz* included Rabbi Elhanan ben Yaher and Rabbi Eliezar of Worms. Both writers were preoccupied with the mystery of God, and were indifferent to philosophical inquiry. They insisted that God could never be known, that only his glory

BELOW: Jews settled all over Eastern Europe. This is the Stara Synagogue in Krakow, Poland which was built by Mateo Gucci in the 1570s.

could be perceived, and that a vision of God could be attained only through a life of devotion, contemplation, and discipline; virtue and piety were of far more consequence than intellectual attainment. Another feature of their writings was an interest in magic. In the Middle Ages Jews had the reputation of being magicians; in particular they practised a technique known as *gematria*, which gave each Hebrew letter a numerical value, so that the total value of sayings and prayers could be calculated to match particular biblical passages. Such prayers were seen as a mystical ascent to God.

During the appalling insecurities of the 12th and 13th centuries, these German mystics offered their followers a sense of purpose and comfort. Death was not to be feared, because martyrdom was the highest honor. God's glory shone through the world, but only through devotion, prayer, perseverance and discipline could the faithful perceive it.

The Zohar and Lurianic Mysticism

Meanwhile, a slightly different mystical tradition was developing in southern France. An important anonymous work, the *Sefer ha-Bahir* (Book of Bahir) pictured God's emanations as crowns or vessels which make up the structure of the divine realm. In the early 13th century, Isaac the Blind (1160-1235) drew on Neoplatonist ideas to argue that the first emanation from God the Infinite was divine thought, and that all the other emanations stemmed from this. He believed that the material world was merely a manifestation of the emanations on a lower scale of reality, and that through contemplation it was possible to ascend the ladder of the emanations to unite oneself with divine thought.

At the same time in northern Spain, Azriel ben Menahem was teaching that divine will rather than divine thought was the first emanation of the Infinite. A mystical school grew up in the town of Gerona, the best-known member of which was Nahmanides (1197-1270) who is primarily remembered as a Jewish philosopher who defended the speculations of Maimonides. However, he was also deeply involved in mystical speculation, and he succeeded in persuading many of his fellow-Jews that such a spiritual quest was compatible with traditional Talmudic scholarship. Other eminent Spanish mystics included Abraham ben Samuel Abulafia (1240-71) and Isaac ibn Latif (1220-90). These mystics knew of the ideas of the Hasidei Ashkenaz in Germany, but they were also influenced by the thinking of the Sufis which they had encountered in Muslim Spain: for example, it was suggested that there were 10 demonic outpourings to parallel God's divine emanations.

Most significant of all these traditions was the appearance of the *Zohar* (literally Divine splendor) at the end of the 13th century, which became the most influential text of the Jewish mystical tradition. It is set in the 2nd century C.E., after the time of the Simeon bar Kokhba revolt, and it focuses on the school of the Mishnaic sage Simeon bar Yohai. It was, in fact, mainly composed by Rabbi Moses de Leon (1250-1305), and was largely based on the teachings of the Gerona school. It identified the 10 emanations of God as being the Supreme Crown, Wisdom, Intelligence, Greatness, Power, Beauty, Endurance, Majesty, Foundation and Kingdom. The first three made up the intellectual realm of the Divine; the second three indicated God's moral qualities; the following three were archetypes for the forces of nature, and the final emanation, Kingdom, was the channel between the Divine and the material spheres. There were attempts to illustrate the emanations as a tree, as 10 concentric spheres or as an archetypal human being. Altogether, the 10 emanations represented the totality of Divine Energy.

The Zohar stressed that the Jewish mystical system was never intended as mere theoretical speculation. It would not only benefit the pious individual who might achieve union with the Divine; it was also thought to bring about cosmic repair to the world. Human action was believed to have a real effect on the higher universe: disharmony had been first brought about by the sin of Adam, but through mystical union, harmony could gradually be restored. These teachings spread through the Jewish world and by the 16th century had become an integral part of the Jewish mind-set; They would bring consolation during difficult times.

By the 15th century a substantial proportion of world Jewry was settled in the territory of the Ottoman Turks. Particularly after the expulsion of the Jews from Spain in 1492, communities were flourishing all over the empire;

Jewish centers in the 16th and 17th century

Jews even rose to important positions in the sultan's court. By this stage, there was an acknowledged difference between the customs of the Jews from Spain and Islamic countries, who were known as the Sephardim, and those of the Jews who came from northern France, Germany and Eastern Europe, who were described as Ashkenazim. Each group had its own distinctive language (Ladino and Yiddish), and there were significant divergencies in the two communities' interpretation of various aspects of the law. When the great Sephardic legal expert, Joseph Caro (1488-1575), published his code of Jewish law, the *Shulhan Arukh* (Prepared Table), the Ashkenazic Moses Isserles (1525-75) had to add a supplement to make it acceptable to his own community. Caro himself had moved to Safed in the Holy Land, which was a center of mystical scholarship; during this period Safed had a population of about 10,000, and the Safed mystics were famous for their ascetic practices. Prominent among them were Moses Cordovero (1522-70) and Isaac Luria (1534-72). Luria, in particular, may be said to have transformed the mystical tradition. He was steeped in the lore of the Zohar and, while he lived in Safed, he surrounded himself with a group of sympathetic disciples who subsequently spread his teaching through the Sephardic world. Luria conjectured that when the Infinite created the universe, He had had to shrink Himself to provide an empty space. So creation was not a positive outpouring, but rather a withdrawal, an exile of God. After the vacuum had been formed, then light flowed from God and took on the shape of the emanation. Each emanation formed a vessel, but so strong was the Divine light that the vessels broke, allowing evil and disaster to enter. The universe became divided between good and evil, and it

RIGHT: The Zohar focused on the school of the Mishnaic sage Simeon bar Yohai whose hiding place this was.

remains a battleground between the two forces; human beings in particular are the focus of the war. The first Adam failed to defeat the evil forces and subsequently the people of Israel were chosen for the task of repairing the world.

Luria believed that he was living in the final days of the struggle, and he was convinced that the long-promised Messiah would soon appear. By the end of the 17th century Messianic speculation was a central feature of the religious life of the Jews of the Ottoman Empire.

Shabbetai Zevi, a Mystical Messiah

In the early 17th century, the Jewish people were enduring a particularly difficult period. Traditionally Poland had been a refuge for the community: Polish nobles had used Jews to run their estates, and had welcomed them into the country. Consequently there was a large Jewish population in Poland, Talmudic studies flourished, and many Jews achieved prosperity and success. However, in 1648 there was a rebellion against the Polish aristocracy. Led by Bogdon Chmielnicki, Cossack hordes set about slaughtering Jews, seeing them as representatives of the hated nobility. All in all, it has been estimated that a quarter of the entire Polish-Jewish community was destroyed in these attacks; Poland was no longer to be seen as a refuge but as a place of terror, insecurity and grief.

Shabbetai Zevi was born in Smyrna in 1626 on the fast day of the ninth of Av (this is the traditional date of birth of the Messiah). He was a gifted scholar who was ordained as a rabbi at the age of 18, after which he devoted himself to mystical study, particularly of the Zohar, and to ascetic exercises, and he attracted a large group of disciples around him. Throughout his life he seems to have been subject to periods of depression, followed by manic euphoria – presumably the accident of his date of birth encouraged his Messianic pretentions. His behavior became increasingly erratic and, in about 1651, he was expelled by the religious authorities from Smyrna. For the next few years he wandered through Greece and Turkey, promulgating his message and shocking pious Jews by his wildness. Following the example of the biblical prophet, Hosea, he married a girl of known immoral behavior who was a survivor of the Chmielnicki massacres and he let it be known that she was the "bride of the Messiah."

The turning point of his career came when he met Nathan of Gaza (1643-80). Nathan, who was himself a brilliant scholar, was convinced that Shabbetai was the Messiah, and he cast himself into the role of the prophet Elijah, the Messianic herald. He sent messages around the entire Jewish world, insisting that the Turkish Sultan would soon be deposed, that the Ten Lost Tribes of Israel would be gathered back from their exile, and that the present disturbances in the world were merely the birth pangs of the Messiah. Since wars of religion were being fought throughout Europe during this period, many in the Jewish community were already convinced that the world was living out its final days; they were looking for a Messiah and, for a time, it seemed as if God had answered their prayers. Jewry was in turmoil and even some rabbinical authorities were carried along in the enthusiasm for Shabbetai. The day of Messianic redemption was set for

June 18, 1666. Throughout Europe penitential dirges were sung in preparation, prayers were said for "Our Lord and King Shabbetai Zevi," traditional fast days were transformed into times of rejoicing and people were even disposing of their property in preparation for the coming golden age.

Shabbetai himself sailed for Constantinople, presumably to depose the Sultan. On landing, however, he was arrested by the Turkish authorities and imprisoned in the fortress of Gallipoli, which was rapidly turned into a Messianic court. Pilgrims traveled from all the corners of the world for audience with Shabbetai, and to receive the Messianic blessing. Although the Turks were reluctant to turn Shabbetai into a martyr, it was clear that imprisonment was doing nothing to lessen his delusions of grandeur. Eventually he was taken to the court of the grand vizier and he was given the choice of being put to death or of converting to Islam. Both Shabbetai and his wife opted for the latter alternative, and he eventually died as an exile in Albania in 1676.

Amazingly, despite his conversion, many of Shabbetai's disciples remained faithful. Nathan himself insisted that Shabbetai's conversion was merely a Messianic exile in which he was battling in the enemy camp with the ultimate forces of evil. By going down into the abyss, the Messiah was liberating divine sparks which would repair the world. Many Jews were not convinced, however, and returned to the rabbinical fold; others insisted that it was not Shabbetai who had become a Muslim, but a phantom – Shabbetai himself had really ascended to heaven. In any event, Shabbeteanism survived in various forms.

In Turkey some believers converted to Islam and formed the Donmeh sect. They retained a separate Jewish life and opposed intermarriage with Muslims, but, at the same time, they rejected much of the Torah and indulged in ritual sexual promiscuity. They had their own places of worship and cemeteries, they devised their own liturgy, and they kept their ancestral Jewish names. A small Donmeh community survived in Istanbul right up to the beginning of the 20th century.

Still more radical were the Frankists. Jacob Frank (1726-91) was influenced by the Donmeh, and believed that he was both a reincarnation of Shabbetai, and the second person of the Trinity. His followers were formally baptized into Roman Catholicism in 1759, but they continued their traditional quasi-Jewish practices in secret. Cult practices involved licentious sexual orgies and secret mystical doctrines. Although Frank himself was imprisoned, this only enhanced his reputation and for a time the sect was extremely successful, many affluent Frankists intermarrying with the Polish aristocracy. None-the-less, the sect had completely died out by the middle of the 19th century.

The excitement generated by Shabbetai Zevi and his followers shook the Jewish community to its foundations and left it profoundly disillusioned. Normative Judaism survived, however, and to this day the pious still await the Messiah, the descendant of King David. As the great philosopher Maimonides declared in one of his principles of the Jewish faith;

"I believe with perfect trust that the Messiah will come, and even though he delays, I will still believe."

Another Polish synagogue — the Nozyk which was the only one to survive the depredations of the Warsaw ghetto during World War II.

The Jews spread out across Europe, establishing themselves in many countries.
RIGHT and BELOW: The kitchen and synagogue in Dublin's Irish Jewish Museum.

OPPOSITE PAGE: ABOVE LEFT and BELOW: The synagogue and cemetery in the Jewish quarter of Prague.

ABOVE RIGHT: The Central Synagogue in Budapest.

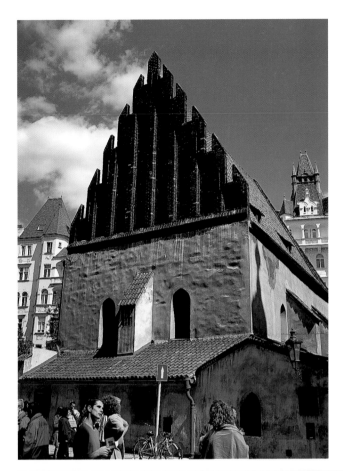

CHAPTER SEVEN

THE HASIDIM

European Jewry at the End of the 17th Century

The Chmielnicki massacres of 1648 had been particularly traumatic for the Jews of Poland; for centuries Polish rulers had provided them with employment and a secure basis for communal existence. Polish Jewry was known for its Talmudic scholarship and for its strict adherence to Jewish law. The community was even allowed a degree of autonomy: from about 1550, the Council of the Four Lands regulated Jewish life throughout Poland and Lithuania. The communal language was Yiddish; the rabbis controlled their own religious law courts; and numerous Talmudic academies had been established.

Between 1400 and 1500 the Jewish population of Poland had increased tenfold. During this period various forms of discrimination were being practised against the community. Jews had to wear distinctive clothing and they were periodically accused of using the blood of Christian children for the making of unleavened bread for Passover. None-the-less theirs was a pious, secure and successful community – until the Chmielnicki massacres upset the equilibrium, and the conversion of Shabbetari Zevi, the self-proclaimed Messiah, to Islam, increased their disillusionment. It was felt that Talmudic scholarship and traditional rabbinical learning had failed them.

During this period, a large proportion of Eastern European Jews lived in the countryside in small towns and villages known as *shtetlach*. A shtetl was a small town with a population between 1,000 and 20,000, the vast majority of whom were Jews. Shtetlach existed not only in Poland, but also in Lithuania, in Austria-Hungary, and in the Russian Pale of Settlement. Vivid pictures of life in these villages can be found in the writings of Sholom Aleichem and in the paintings of Marc Chagall. The popularity of the musicals *Yentl* and *Fiddler on the Roof*, both based on stories by Sholom Aleichem, shows the nostalgia that still exists for the Shtetl way of life, which was characterized by *Yiddishkeit* (Jewishness) and *menschlikheit* (humanity). The synagogue was the central institution; men and women prayed separately in different parts of the building, and everyone knew their place through the hierarchy of the seating: the rich and respected within the community sat near the Ark, while the disreputable and the unsuccessful were confined to areas near the door. At home the mother reigned supreme: she lit the Sabbath candles, prepared the kosher food and brought up the children. Marriages were arranged by a professional matchmaker and were seen as alliances between families. Everyone knew everyone else's business; privacy was not a meaningful concept, and the entire community was closely involved in the affairs of each individual family. People lived their lives guided by the old rituals and sustained by their neighbors.

If at all possible, the sons of the family were educated in a yeshiva, under the supervision of a prominent rabbi. They primarily studied the Talmud, and their education was intended to encourage a lifelong devotion to study, providing a glimpse of the joys of being immersed in the laws of God. Later, throughout their lives, Jewish men would gather in the study hall attached to the synagogue to continue their studies after their day's work was finished. Meanwhile, the girls were taught housewifery and all the other essential elements that went into the making of a good Jewish wife and mother. Families were large and, despite poverty and hardship, the Jewish community was notably more healthy and better educated than their gentile neighbours. In any event, contact with outsiders was to be avoided if at all possible: particularly after the Chmielnicki massacres, any interaction might all too easily end in a riot, a pogram or even another massacre.

The situation in Western Europe was different. Until the end of the 17th century, the Jews lived in societies where little had changed since the Middle Ages. Monarchs still believed that they ruled by Divine Right; the Christian church still controlled most educational institutions and, in general, the Jews were confined to special areas of residence and were expected to wear distinctive clothing. There were, however, notable exceptions: in neither England nor the Netherlands did the government interfere with the life of the community, and in Holland, in particular, the community was affluent and powerful. However, elsewhere change was in the air. In the Holy Roman Empire in 1781, under the enlightened Emperor Joseph II (1741-90), the Jewish badge was abolished and an Edict of Toleration was issued; Jews were permitted to send their children to secular schools, and were given the freedom to engage in trade and industry.

Similar reforms took place in France. After the French Revolution, the Assembly of Notables laid down that no one should be persecuted for their religious opinions, and in 1791, the Assembly granted full citizenship to Jews. When Napoleon became Emperor of France in 1804, he established the right of every French citizen to follow any trade. In 1806 he took the extraordinary step of convening an Assembly of Jewish Notables to enquire whether Jewish law was compatible with French law, and whether French Jews could also be loyal French citizens. When reassured on this point, in 1807 he revived the Sanhedrin. He called together a gathering of rabbis and prominent laymen who pledged their allegiance to the emperor. From that time on, the French-Jewish community was organized in much the same way as any other branch of the civil service.

Inevitably, after the Battle of Waterloo and the defeat of Napoleon, there was an attempt by the great European powers to turn back the clock: in 1819, for example, there were some serious anti-Jewish riots in several German cities. None-the-less, liberalism was in the air. Many prominent German intellectuals, such as Gabriel Riesser (1806-63) and Heinrich Heine (1797-1856), began to argue for the rights of Jews. After the revolutions of 1848, increased freedoms of speech, assembly and religion were granted, and by 1871 all restrictions on Jewish life had been removed. Jews had become full citizens of the new German Second Reich. In England, religious tests were gradually being abolished, generally in response to particular cases. The first Jew became Sheriff of London in

Hasidic Jews at the Wailing Wall in Jerusalem

1835; in 1858 the first Jew formally took his seat as a Member of Parliament, and the Board of Deputies of British Jews received its first constitution in 1836.

Thus in Western Europe, in contrast to the East, Jews were far more likely to receive a secular education, to participate in gentile activities and to join mainstream society. Assimilation became a real threat, and traditional pious Orthodoxy was no longer spiritually satisfying to many.

Hasidism

After the horrors of the Chmielnicki massacres and the debacle of Shabbetai Zevi the false Messiah, the Jewish villages of Eastern Europe turned to a new religious movement. Its founder was Israel ben Eliezer (*c.* 1700-60) who was known as the *Baal Shem Tov* (the Master of the Good Name), or the *Besht*. Biographical details are scanty; he was probably born in the Carpathian Mountains in the village of Okup and he seems, in the early days, to have earned his living by working as a religious slaughterer and teacher. He rapidly became known as a miracle worker and he gathered a group of disciples around him. The Besht himself left no writings, but his teachings were preserved and subsequently published in Hebrew (presumably he had originally spoken to his followers in Yiddish).

His emphasis was always on the joy of serving God. The Besht was not remarkable for his learning or his scholarship, although there are several legends of his getting the better of established scholars. Instead he insisted that the study of the Law should be a matter not of the intellect, but of religious devotion. He believed that every detail of daily life, from getting up in the morning to going to bed at night, should be performed in a spirit of joy and worship. He was also known for his dedication to prayer: his disciples observed how he would make wild gestures when he prayed to God, as an expression of his longing. He himself used to say that a drowning man is not ashamed to wave and gesticulate in order to be rescued; similarly he would desperately wave his arms so that he might be saved by God.

After the Besht's death, the movement which he had initiated swept through Poland and beyond. His followers were known as the Hasidim (pious ones), and they studied their leader's maxims as expressed in the work *Tolodot Ya'akov Yosef* (Generations of Jacob Joseph), which had been compiled by his disciple Jacob Joseph of Polonnoye (*c.* 1710-72). Other prominent early leaders of Hasidism included Dov Baer the Maggid (Preacher) of Mezhirech (1710-72), Levi Yitshak of Berdichev (*c.* 1740-1810), Shneur Zalman of Lyady (1745-1813), Elimelech of Lyzhansk (1717-87) and the Besht's great-grandson, the storyteller, Nahman of Bratslav (1772-1811). East European Jewry was quickly infected with Hasidic ideas: the verse from the biblical Book of Genesis, "A river flowed out of Eden to water the garden; it then divided to become four branches" was interpreted to refer to the passing of the movement from Dov Baer to Elimelech of Lyzhansk through to four further prominent disciples.

Although in the early days the leadership was passed from master to disciple, it soon became a matter of dynastic descent. Leadership was central to the philosophy of the Hasidim and the leader of the particular Hasidic group was known as the *Zaddik* (righteous one). The notion of a Zaddik is an ancient one in Judaism; according to the Talmud, the very existence of the world rests upon the righteousness of the 36 Zaddikim. The early mystics had taught that the Zaddik had divine power and must be seen as a channel through which God communicated with His people. The Hasidim therefore treated their particular Zaddik with utmost reverence.

The movement quickly split between the followers of particular Zaddikim. Each group maintained their Zaddik in a court, and some Zaddikim lived in conditions of considerable opulence. Even today, members of Hasidic sects visit their Zaddik and observe his behavior as a pattern to be followed. For example, there is a famous anecdote about a disciple of the Maggid of Mezhirech who went to see his master not to learn about Jewish law, nor to receive his blessing, but to observe how he tied his shoes! By watching the Zaddik, it was thought possible to learn how God can be worshiped in every moment of daily life. Today the Zaddik gives mass audiences in his court; he is available to give individuals spiritual advice, and he is maintained financially by his community. When the Zaddik presides over a communal meal, the greatest compliment is to be given a piece of food from the master's own hands. Even his leftovers are seized eagerly by his followers, since eating food which has been touched by the Zaddik is believed to aid spirituality.

Hasidism may have been a new approach to Judaism, but it was derived from the Bible, rabbinical literature and the mystical tradition. It must be seen as a reaction to the cerebral nature of traditional Jewish learning; enthusiasm and joy were to be emphasized instead. The Besht himself used to say, "What matters is not how many precepts you fulfill, but the spirit in which you fulfill them." Modern Hasidic worship remains notable for its devotion and fervor, and the Hasidim still believe that God is to be found in every detail of life and in every corner of the universe. Every moment can, and should, be dedicated to the service and worship of the Master of the Universe.

Hasidic sects still flourish today, even though the communities of Eastern Europe were decimated in the Holocaust. None-the-less, there are sizeable groups located particularly in Israel and the United States. The Zaddik is now generally called *rebbe* (teacher) or, in Israel, *admor* (an acoustic meaning, our Lord, our teacher, our rabbi). Members of the Hasidic groups wear distinctive dress: the men black hats, black suits with visible ritual fringes, and sport beards and side-curls; the women dress modestly and married women wear a wig to fulfill the injunction to cover one's head at all times. Men and women marry young and large families are regarded as a blessing. On the Sabbath in the Hasidic areas of big cities, mothers and fathers with seven or eight children may frequently be seen out walking. Their rebbes are the direct spiritual (and physical) descendants of the Zaddikim of the late 18th century. Among the best-known groups are the Lubavich, the Satmar, the Belz, the Bobover and the Gur. They are named after the original East European villages from which they originated, and they all support their own courts and religious institutions.

Hasidic sects still flourish today, even though the communities of Eastern Europe were decimated in the Holocaust. Members of the Hasidic groups wear distinctive dress: the men black hats, black suits with visible ritual fringes, and sport beards and side-curls; the women dress modestly and married women wear a wig to fulfill the injunction to cover one's head at all times.

The Mitnagdim

In spite of the attractions of Hasidism, not all the rabbinical authorities of Eastern Europe were in favor of the new movement. In fact, in the early years, there was constant conflict between the Hasidim and the mainstream leaders. The Hasidim, for example, did not use the traditional Ashkenazi (East European) prayer book. Instead they adopted a new prayer rite, which was largely based on the Sephardic (Spanish) version used by the mystic, Isaac Luria. They also restricted themselves to their own ritual slaughterers and created a separate industry of supervision, which undermined the traditional structures. In addition, mainstream rabbis, who were steeped in Talmudic learning, were suspicious of the miraculous tales told of the Zaddikim, and were scornful of the many collections of their homilies produced by their disciples. Thus the rabbinical establishment became determined to fight back and to reassert its authority throughout Poland, Lithuania, Russia and Austria-Hungary.

The term *Mitnagdim* simply means "opponents." It was the name given to those who disliked the exuberance and the anti-intellectualism of the Hasidim. In the beginning, the Mitnagdim feared that the enthusiasm of the Hasidim would lead to similarly disastrous results as had Shabbetai Zevi's popular Messianism. The community had been shattered by the disappointment of Shabbetai's conversion to Islam, and the appearance of licentious fringe groups such as the Donmeh and the Frankists that emerged after the catastrophe was scarcely reassuring; the Mitnagid rabbis feared that Hasidic enthusiasm would lead to similar excesses. They were appalled by the Hasidic abandonment of the traditional Ashkenazi prayer book, and they deplored the setting up of small Hasidic houses of worship separate from the mainstream synagogues. They could not accept the Hasidic neglect of painstaking Talmudic scholarship, and they emphatically rejected the veneration of the Zaddikim.

The stronghold of the Mitnagdim was Lithuania and the community of its capital, Vilna, was famous for being the most learned in Eastern Europe – even today "as clever as a Litvak" is a simile used in the Jewish community. The leading Talmudist of his time, Elijah ben Solomon Zalman (1720-97), roused his fellow Jews of Vilna to take a stand against the new movement.

Elijah himself was a remarkable person: known as the *Vilna Gaon*, his outstanding scholarship was admired throughout the Jewish world. His great intellect had been recognized from a very early age. According to legend, he gave his first sermon in the Great Synagogue of Vilna at the age of six. By the time he was 13, the traditional age of bar mitzvah, or coming of age, he was regarded as an authority in both the Talmudic and the mystical tradition. Following the customs of East European Jewry he married young and, after his marriage, traveled extensively throughout the Jewish world. When he was 25, he returned to the city of Vilna and initially lived there as a recluse. Although his learning and sanctity were recognized by the community and he was supported by a small pension from communal funds, he lived on the outskirts of the city. He is said to have slept for only two hours every night and, in order to stay awake, would regularly plunge his feet in a pail of cold water. Wrapped in his prayer shawl, he devoted himself to prayer and study. He never even went to synagogue, saying that he preferred to pray at home because in the synagogue it was impossible to avoid hearing idle gossip.

At the age of 40, after 15 years, he emerged from his seclusion. He admitted a small group of disciples, all of whom were distinguished scholars in their own right, to his inner circle, and he determined to stand out against Hasidism. He insisted, as a matter of principle, that the only things worth having were obtained through hard labor. He mistrusted the easy exuberance of the followers of Hasidism, and was convinced that it undermined serious and determined Talmudic scholarship. He refused even to visit those Hasidic leaders who were anxious to talk with him, and he conducted ceremonial burnings of Hasidic books. He went so far as to pronounce a ban of excommunication against those who joined Hasidic groups. The conflict was extremely acrimonious. So fervent was the anti-Hasidic feeling that families became divided. If a son joined a Hasidic group, it was not uncommon for his parents to cut him out of their lives and to perform the traditional rites of mourning, just as if he had died. In general, however, the communities of Lithuania followed Elijah's lead, but the struggle between the Hasidim and the Mitnagdim continued even after Elijah's death. So embittered were both sides, that on one occasion they even appealed to the secular Russian authorities against each other.

Elijah himself was highly influential in the revival of Talmudic scholarship: he is often called the "Father of Talmud criticism," and he wrote over 70 books. He disapproved of the traditional hair-splitting method of scholarship (known as *pilpul*), in which disparate texts were put together and were then forced into a relationship. Instead he delved ceaselessly into the works of early authorities, and he regarded the Palestinian Talmud as being of equal importance as the Babylonian. His annotations of the Talmud are still printed in standard editions alongside the original text. In addition, partly through his influence, the old method of study in the Talmudic academies was modified.

Later, ethics was added to the curriculum in Lithuania. This addition was largely the work of Israel Lipkin (1810-83), another native of Vilna. He believed that there was too much emphasis on the ritual precepts of Judaism, and that the academies could encourage improved standards of behavior in their students specifically through the study of ethical texts.

All the Jewish institutions of Eastern Europe were undermined in the late 19th century, partly as a result of the economic difficulties of the time. In addition, there was a considerable threat from the values of the secular Enlightenment which was permeating through from Western Europe. Both the Hasidim and the Mitnagdim recognized the danger; by the end of the 19th century, they had largely buried their differences: together they stood firm for the values of traditional Orthodoxy against the creeping influence of secular liberalism.

The Enlightenment

While the Hasidim and Mitnagdim were battling it out in Eastern Europe, momentous changes were occurring in the West. *Haskalah* is the term used for the Jewish Enlightenment, the roots of which go back to the Netherlands of the 17th century. The synagogues of that period are still standing in Amsterdam today: they are large and magnificent buildings, and give some idea of the size and wealth of the community of that period. The foundations had been laid by refugees fleeing Spain during the great expulsion of 1492; their coreligionists, who had supposedly converted to Christianity in order to remain in their homes, were subsequently forced to leave for more hospitable countries in the 16th and 17th centuries and swelled the numbers of the Amsterdam community, bringing a rich tradition with them. These, of course, were Sephardic Jews but, there was also an Ashkenazic group which followed the Eastern European traditions. Many of its members were refugees from the Chmielnicki massacres and other persecutions.

Thus Amsterdam became a major Jewish center. There were several important Jewish publishers; there was a famous Talmud-Torah school, and the congregation included physicians, dramatists, merchants and bankers. Even a cursory glance at the surviving engravings of the congregation shows a group of affluent individuals dressed in the latest fashions.

The most famous of the Dutch thinkers of this period was the philosopher Baruch Spinoza (1632-77), the descendant of a Portuguese refugee family. His philosophy was greatly influenced by that of René Descartes, and he was a true man of his times – rational, observant and open to new ideas. In his *Theological Political Treatise* he suggested that Moses did not compose the entire Torah – this so incensed the community that he was completely rejected from the synagogue. Never-the-less, although his works were banned as heretical by the Jewish establishment, they provided a background to the philosophical ideas of Moses Mendelssohn (1729-86).

Moses Mendelssohn lived in Berlin, and must be seen as the most significant figure of the Haskalah. He was encouraged in his work by his close friend, the Christian philosopher and dramatist, G. E. Lessing – indeed, Mendelssohn was almost certainly the model for the main character in Lessing's *Nathan the Wise*. Mendelssohn was convinced that all the essentials of the Jewish religion – the existence of God, the immortality of the human soul and the nature of divine providence – could be discovered by unaided human reason. In his *Jerusalem*, he articulated the Jewish mission to the world as calling "wholesome and unadulterated ideas of God and his attributes continuously to the attention of the rest of mankind." He argued for the separation of the state from religion, and for freedom of worship. He continually worked for the betterment of his people, and he was a loyal and respected member of Berlin's Jewish community.

On one occasion Mendelssohn was publicly challenged by the Swiss clergyman, J. K. Lavater, to disprove the truth of Christianity or to convert. Such an idea was repugnant to him, and he used to say that he could not understand how those who were born into the household of Jacob could in good conscience exempt themselves from the observance of the Law. Yet he was determined to help his coreligionists participate in mainstream Western culture, for he realized that Jews must be comfortable with the modern world if they were to become part of it. He therefore translated the Pentateuch into German and he added to his translation a biblical commentary, which was largely based on the classical commentaries, but which gave his fellow-Germans a rational explanation of Jewish law; it was much used and highly influential. In addition, Mendelssohn believed that traditional Jewish education had to be modernized. He supported the setting up of a Jewish Free School in Berlin in 1781, and similar schools were built in other Jewish centers which taught secular subjects as well as the Talmud. Mendelssohn's followers were enthusiastic about these projects, and produced the first Jewish literary magazine devoted to the introduction of the Jewish people to secular culture.

Mendelssohn himself was highly respected in both the Jewish and the Christian communities, and he remained Orthodox in his observance of the Jewish law throughout his life. However, his own family history illustrates the conflict contained in the Jewish emancipation: of his six children, no less than four subsequently converted to Christianity later in their lives (the composer Felix Mendelssohn was his grandson). This was to become the all-too-frequent experience of 19th-century Jews influenced by the Enlightenment.

By the 1820s, the center of the Haskalah movement had transferred to Vienna. This was the city in which the two periodicals, *First Fruit of the Times* and *Vineyard of Delight* were published and came to be the main promulgators of Haskalah views. The ideas of their writers can be summarized as the conviction that secular studies had to be part of the education of every Jewish child if they were to take advantage of the benefits of the modern world. Furthermore, Jews should be thoroughly familiar with the language of secular society: thus they should be educated in German, French, Dutch or whatever their country's *lingua franca* happened to be, but not in Yiddish. Hebrew rather than Yiddish was the traditional language of the Jews, and should therefore be used to revive a Jewish sense of nationhood. The Jewish religion itself must adapt to the situation of human beings in the modern world (this was to lead to both the Reform and the Neo-orthodox movements, both of which will be explored later in the chapter). Finally, they believed that the Jews must work toward having their own homeland and must cease to be a nation in exile. This conviction would give rise to Zionism and finally to the creation of the state of Israel in the 20th century.

The Haskalah must thus be seen as the origin of many of the important trends in modern Judiasm. It is difficult to know, however, whether or not it strengthened the community. On the one hand, many, like Mendelssohn's children, identified so strongly with mainstream culture that they abandoned their religion altogether. On the other, many Jews only remained within the fold because they could find a Judaism which was compatible with their view of the world within the thought of the Haskalah.

The Reform Movement

One result of the Haskalah was that many West European Jews felt that the traditional forms of Jewish worship were no longer relevant to their lives. The first Reform temple was built in Sesen as a result of this. Instead of the old forms of Hebrew prayer, much of the liturgy was in German, and choral singing was introduced. This temple was transferred to Berlin after Napoleon's occupation, and another important congregation was founded in Hamburg in 1818 – this latter group went so far as to issue its own prayer book. All the prayers invoking the restoration of Zion and the coming of the Messiah were omitted, and repetitions were excised. Members of the new movement were anxious to take part in mainstream secular culture and they wanted to be good Germans; there could be no question of a dual loyalty for such modern Jews.

In the 19th century, a number of Christian theologians were beginning to examine their own tradition objectively without the hindrance of any preconceived religious bias; the same was happening in Judaism. Among such scholars it could no longer be taken for granted that God gave the Pentateuch and the entire oral law to Moses on Mount Sinai; such authorities as Leopold Zunz (1794-1886) believed that the Jewish religion, like everything else, was subject to the historical process. In the middle of the 19th century, the two Christian scholars, Julius Wellhausen and Heinrich Graf, concluded that the Five Books of Moses must originally have been compiled from at least four different sources. Jews who had been educated in the secular world were very often convinced by such arguments; for many it was no longer possible to believe that the Law had been divinely revealed in its perfect entirety.

A central figure in the new Reform movement was Abraham Geiger (1810-74), the rabbi of Breslau, who formulated the principles on which Reform Judaism would rest, for if the Law was not divinely revealed by God, it could clearly be modified. He believed that the essence of Judaism lay not in obedience to the law, but in ethical monotheism. His contemporary Samuel Holdheim went even further, recommending that the Sabbath be transferred from Saturday to Sunday to fit in with mainstream custom, and that the dietary laws be modified.

The new movement spread rapidly, for it was immensely appealing to German Jews who were steeped in Western European culture, but who wanted to retain their Jewish roots. A new rabbinical seminary was founded in Breslau in 1854 at which regular conferences were held during which sympathetic rabbis could discuss such matters as the role of Hebrew in the liturgy, the dietary laws, Sabbath observance and the status of marriage between Jews and Christians. The movement spread to England, where the West London Synagogue for Reform Jews was found in 1841, and to Hungary, where a moderate Reform Rabbinical College was opened in 1867. In 1872 the most famous Reform College of all, the Berlin *Hochschule* was set up in 1872, under the direction of Abraham Geiger. In 1899 the Union of Liberal Rabbis of Germany was created.

Reform ideas were taken across the Atlantic Ocean to America by

German immigrants. In 1845 Temple Emmanuel was founded in New York City which used the new patterns of worship; the first conference of American Reform Rabbis took place in Philadelphia in 1869; and the first American Rabbinical Seminary was founded in Cincinnati by Rabbi Isaac Meyer Wise (1819-1900). Wise, a man of enormous energy, also started two periodicals, one in English and one in German, and produced a new prayer book, the *Minhag America* (American Custom).

Under the direction of Kaufman Kohler (1843-1926), the principles of the new movement were debated and, in 1885, a formal Reform platform was produced. It was agreed that, in view of the findings of scientists, historians and biblical critics, Jewish law had to be modified. Although the moral regulations were valid for all time, only the rituals which were regarded as being spiritually uplifting should be retained: the dietary laws, the laws of dress and the laws of ritual purity need no longer be observed. It was felt that it was no longer realistic to look for the coming of a personal Messiah, nor to expect the resurrection of the body, nor everlasting reward and punishment. Instead Reform Jews should work for the establishment of justice and peace in this world, should be committed to social action, and should build up a progressive religion.

Orthodox Jews were appalled by these developments. In the early days there had been attempts to shut down the Berlin temple. Several harsh rabbinical decrees had also been issued against the Reformers: for example, the rabbinic court of Prague declared: "It is their entire desire to parade before the Christians as being more learned than their brothers. Basically they have no religion at all." From the beginning of the Haskalah, many traditional Jews feared any form of emancipation, and saw that increased familiarity with mainstream culture would inevitably lead to temptation. Their fears were, to some extent, realized by the conversion to Christianity of several prominent Jews of the time.

However, a few Orthodox thinkers were prepared to make some accommodation of the modern world. Foremost among them was Rabbi Samson Raphael Hirsch (1808-88) who had had both a secular and a rabbinic education. In 1836 he published a defence of traditional Judaism entitled *The Nineteen Letters on Judaism*, in which he argued that the mission of the Jewish people was to illustrate to the rest of the world the joy that is to be found in obedience to the Law. But, he stressed, leading an Orthodox life did not preclude the possibility of being conversant with modern culture. This position came to be known as Neo-orthodoxy and meant that while there could be no compromise on the doctrine of God's Law being given to Moses, at the same time Jews could have the benefit of a secular education.

Thus, by the middle of the 19th century, many Jews had become indistinguishable from their fellow-citizens in Western Europe and in the US: eating the same food, practising no unusual customs and enjoying full civil rights. Others retained the old ways, but still took part in the modern world. In Eastern Europe, little had changed in the old Jewish villages: for them life continued in the old way until the end of the century. Change would not be prompted by political emancipation, but as a response to anti-Semitism and by the lure of opportunities from across the Atlantic Ocean.

CHAPTER EIGHT

ANTI-SEMITISM AND ZIONISM

The Anti-Jewish Tradition in Christian Europe

Hatred of the Jews has a long history. The Christian church has, from its beginnings, believed itself to be the authentic heir of God's promises to the patriarch Abraham. When the Jews failed to recognize Jesus as the long-awaited Messiah, they were regarded as having been rejected by God. This animosity was fueled by New Testament writers, who placed the blame for the death of Jesus firmly on the shoulders of the Jewish people. Indeed, the Evangelists go out of their way to exonerate the Roman civil authority and to place the responsibility on the Jews – even though the final decision as to the execution rested with the Roman governor.

Following the New Testament tradition, the church fathers continued the vilification of the Jews. To take one example among many, St. John Chrysostom wrote, "The synagogue is not only a whorehouse and a theater; it is also a den of thieves and a haunt of wild animals . . . not the cave of a wild animal merely, but of an unclean wild animal . . . The Jews have no conception of things at all, but living for the lower nature, all agog for the here and now, no better disposed than pigs or goats, they live by the rule of debauchery and inordinate gluttony . . ."

Because they had rejected the salvation offered in Jesus, it was thought permissible to treat the Jews badly. As Hippolytus put it in his *Expository Treatise Against the Jews*. "Hear this yet more serious word: 'And their back do thou bend down always.' That means in order that they may be slaves to the nations, not 400 years as in Egypt, or 70 years as in Babylon, but bend them in servitude, he says, always."

Throughout the Middle Ages, particularly at the time of the Crusades, there were Jewish persecutions. So, for example, in 1473 nine Jews in the Austrian Tyrol were tortured until they confessed to killing a Christian boy. From the 13th century, Jews were expected to wear distinctive clothing in Christian countries, and on several occasions, after formal disputations between Jewish and Christian scholars, the Talmud was publicly condemned and burned.

During this period the stereotype of the demonic Jew became a part of Western culture. The Jew was portrayed as the personification of evil, and was considered relegated to a subspecies of the human race. Increasingly among the uneducated masses the Jewish population was perceived as possessing the attributes of both the devil and of witches. They were said to grow horns and tails; their beards were likened to the beards of goats, and they were thought to emit a horrible smell. They were all believed to be afflicted with hemorrhoids, and their men, as well as their women, were said to suffer from menstrual periods; tales were told of how they dabbled in the occult and associated with demons. In view of this, many church leaders actively encouraged Jewish persecution. Inevitably, in view of their hardships, the Jews turned in on themselves and formed their own closed world. Some countries, such as England, had expelled the Jews completely; in other places the Jews lived in closed ghettos, the gates of which were locked at night. They lived in fear of their Christian neighbors, and inevitably found their only consolation in their own society and the practice of their religion.

The Protestant Reformation brought little relief. Martin Luther initially condemned the persecution of the Jews and advocated tolerance; however, when the community was not persuaded by his preaching, he turned against them. in his pamphlet *Against the Jews and their Lies*, he wrote,

"First their synagogues should be set on fire . . . Secondly, their homes should be likewise broken down and destroyed . . . Thirdly, they should be deprived of their prayer books and Talmuds . . . Fourthly, their rabbis must be forbidden on pain of death to preach any more . . . Fifthly, passport and traveling privileges should be absolutely forbidden to the Jews . . . Sixthly, they ought to be stopped from usury . . . Seventhly, let the young and strong Jews and Jewesses be given the flail, the ax, the hoe, the spade, the distaff, and spindle and let them earn their bread by the sweat of their noses."

Again he insisted that they were in league with the devil: "In short the Jews are worse than devils. O God, my beloved Father and Creator, have pity on me who, in self-defense, must speak so scandalously of thy divine and eternal Majesty, against thy wicked enemies, the devils and the Jews."

This was the heritage of Christian Europe. But, by the second half of the 19th century, Jewish life in Western Europe had been transformed. Jews were no longer visibly distinctive, they mingled freely with their gentile neighbors, and they played a full part in the cultural and political life of their host nations. Most reformers believed that anti-Jewish sentiment was a thing of the past. Sadly this was not to be the case: the old tradition had survived.

19th-Century Anti-Semitism

Despite their emancipation, for a variety of reasons further hostility toward the Jewish community emerged at the end of the 19th century. The term "anti-Semitism" was first coined in the 1870s by a German journalist named Wilhelm Marr, whose conception was very different from historic anti-Jewish feeling. In the past, Jewish hatred had been justified on religious grounds: Jews had rejected the salvation offered in Jesus; they were said to be Christ-killers and, because of their blind obstinacy, they were condemned to eternal damnation. However, if Jews converted to Christianity, all doors were opened to them; many of those Jews of Christian Spain who were baptized attained high positions of state. When the *Marranos* (converted Jews) were finally expelled from Spain, it was only because they were suspected of harboring their old Jewish practices in secret. Those who fully turned to Christianity were completely accepted.

Marr, however, saw things differently. He insisted that anti-Semitism was nothing to do with religion, and that the Jews were a biologically alien people. They could not be assimilated into mainstream society because they were of a different and foreign race. In fact, he interpreted the whole course of modern history as an ongoing struggle between native Teutonic stock and the "Semitic alien." This biological justification for prejudice against the Jews was unfortunately to become all too influential in the next century. In the 1870s, conditions in Europe were very unsettled: the old empires were weakened and several new nations emerged, all of which were determined to assert their own individual national identity. As a result, indigenous minority groups of all kinds were subject to persecution because they were perceived as a threat to the ruling majority; in these countries, Jews particularly were regarded as foreign intruders.

The situation was notably acute in Germany. In the liberal climate of the mid-19th century many Jews had done well: they had enjoyed the benefits of a secular education and had achieved considerable success in banking, the arts and the commercial world. In 1878, a Christian socialist party was founded; part of its program was that the German press and financial institutions were controlled by Jews, and that therefore the Jews were responsible for all the nation's current problems. This argument was very attractive to the German lower middle classes, for it gave the artisans, the shopkeepers and the clerks a definite scapegoat for their ills. By 1881, it was being publicly claimed that the Jewish physical type constituted a biological threat to the purebred Teutonic nations; cartoons of the period show Jews as gross, hook-nosed, dark, overfed and satanic. Petitions were organized to prevent any further Jewish immigration, and by the 1890s six members of the German Reichstag had been elected to their seats on an anti-Semitic ticket.

Things were not much better in France where, in the past, anti-Jewish feeling had from time to time been exploited by the monarchists and clergy to counter liberalism. But it was the Dreyfus case which brought the latent anti-Semitism of the nation to the world's attention. Captain Alfred Dreyfus (1859-1935) was an officer in the French Army, and the only Jew on the army's senior staff. In 1894 it became clear that someone was betraying information to the German military attaché in Paris, and there was some handwritten evidence to link it with Dreyfus. He was arrested and, despite the fact that the evidence against him was decidedly flimsy, he was court-martialed, convicted and sentenced to life imprisonment. The French intelligentsia were sharply divided regarding the case: some saw Dreyfus as a Jew and therefore almost certainly a traitor, while others perceived him as an innocent man, who was being victimized as he was a member of a minority group.

Then, in 1896, it was discovered that a fellow-officer of Dreyfus, one Ferdinand Esterházy, had been selling secrets to the Germans. But, instead of accepting that there had been a gross miscarriage of justice, the evidence against Esterházy was ignored, and Dreyfus was transferred to a prison in

Tunisia. Meanwhile, outside the army, the campaign to free Dreyfus was gaining momentum. In a panic, the army had Esterházy's accuser arrested for a breach of security and Esterházy himself was acquitted at a court-martial. In an outraged reaction to this, the eminent French novelist, Émile Zola, published his famous article *J'accuse* (I Accuse) in the French newspaper *l'Aurore*, in which he described the Dreyfus trial as a "crime of high treason against humanity." The authorities promptly had Zola arrested on a charge of libel, and he was sentenced to a year's imprisonment. But the campaign could not be silenced and the Dreyfus case went to appeal; in 1899, Dreyfus was tried again. Again, despite the almost complete lack of evidence, he was convicted, but "with extenuating circumstances," and was sentenced to 10 years' imprisonment. Then, 10 days later, the government, without exonerating him, or in any way apologizing, issued a free pardon. Dreyfus was released, and Esterházy committed suicide.

Dreyfus returned to the army and resumed his duties, although he was not fully vindicated until 1906. The whole case caused a sensation in France. Many of the "anti-Dreyfusards" were leading anti-Semites: the journalist, Eduard Drumont, for example, argued in his newspaper *Libre Parole* that the Jews were aiming to take over France. Charles Maurras, who campaigned vigorously against Dreyfus, was a founder of the French fascist movement, Action Française, and would welcome Hitler's occupation of France as a "heavenly surprise." On the other side, the whole affair persuaded some young Jews that the Jewish people could never be safe without a country of their own. Theodor Herzl (1806-1904), the convener of the Zionist Conferences, attended the Dreyfus trial, and the experience persuaded him that, so ingrained was anti-Semitism in Christian culture, there could be no final home for the Jews in Europe.

Pograms and Emigration

Anti-semitism was not restricted to Western Europe: in Russia it had become official state policy. Czar Alexander II had been assassinated in 1881; in response, the Russian authorities cut back on the Jewish right of residence in the Pale of Settlement. By the late 1880s, a quota system had been introduced which restricted Jewish entry into secondary education. In St. Petersburg and Moscow only 3 percent of students in secondary schools could be of Jewish origin; in other major cities the figure was 5 percent. Jewish admission to the universities and the professions was also substantially cut back. During his lifetime Czar Alexander II had initiated several reforms, including, for the first time, allowing certain categories of Jews to live outside the Pale of Settlement. After his assassination all these measures were rescinded and, in 1891, more than 20,000 Jews were expelled from Moscow.

In addition, anti-Semitic literature was being published and circulated. The most famous example was the anonymous *Protocols of the Elders of Zion*, which was known about in Russian official circles from the late 1880s, and which was actually published in a Russian newspaper in 1903. The *Protocols* claimed to be the documents of a mythical council of Jewish elders who were bent on world domination; using the financial institutions and the press, the council intended to take over the government of the world. The work was apparently submitted for the approval of Czar Nicholas II, who rejected it, feeling that it was too obvious a forgery. However, it has been frequently reprinted, and remains in circulation in many countries even today. Recently it has enjoyed a revival in the newly independent states of the old Soviet Union, and is much read throughout the Arab world.

After the death of Czar Alexander II, a new and devastating threat appeared as his successor, Czar Alexander III authorized bands of Cossacks to sweep through the Ukraine and to attack both Jewish people and property. The rumor was circulated that the Jews had, in some way, been responsible for the Czar's assassination, and that this justified the carnage. in Kiev, the capital of the Ukraine, rioting against the Jewish community lasted for three days before the official police thought to interfere. The riots spread through Belorussia and Lithuania, and there was a serious disturbance in Warsaw, the capital of Poland, on Christmas Day 1881. Ultimately the authorities did take measures against the rioters, but they also, at the same time, substantially curtailed Jewish freedoms.

It was during this period that the term "pogrom" entered the Russian language; it is defined in the *American Heritage Dictionary* as an "organized and often officially encouraged massacre or persecution of a minority group, especially . . . the Jews." Fundamentally, it was an attack on one sector of society by another, and it was accompanied by rape, murder and the wanton destruction of property. Pograms were carried out against other groups, such as the Armenians, but, as the dictionary definition indicates, the term is usually applied to attacks against the Jews. At the end of the 19th and beginning of the 20th centuries Russiawas in a state of political turmoil, and the outbreaks of violence were generally linked to social upheaval and nationalist aspirations. Increasingly many in the Jewish community felt that there was no place for them in the country and began to look to a new life in the United States as the only long-term solution to their problems.

A second wave of pogroms took place after Russia's disastrous war with Japan from 1904 to 1905. This was again a time of revolutionary agitation against the government, and increasingly the authorities permitted the popular press to express virulent anti-Semitic sentiments in order to divert the attention of the public from the need for reform. This attitude encouraged pogroms and, on one occasion, more than 300 Jews were killed in Odessa; 45 Jews were murdered in Kishinev, and about 1,500 Jewish houses were looted. Indeed, there was unrest through the whole Pale of Settlement. Still more serious, however, were the outbreaks that took place after World War I. At this time the whole of Russia had been plunged into civil war, and Jews were being targeted by both the Ukrainian units of the Red Army and the counter-revolutionaries of the White Army. Pogroms occurred in every region from the Ukraine to Siberia, and it is estimated that 150,000 died in the onslaught. The news inevitably leaked to the outside world; the Jewish communities of Western Europe and the United States were understandably appalled, and there is no doubt that these outbreaks converted many to the Zionist cause.

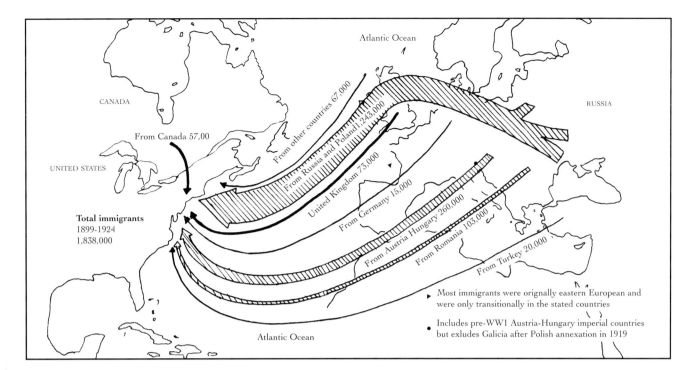

Total immigrants
1899-1924
1,838,000

Most immigrants were orignally eastern European and
were only transitionally in the stated countries

Includes pre-WW1 Austria-Hungary imperial countries
but exludes Galicia after Polish annexation in 1919

Thus, for most Jews at the end of the 19th century, the promised land was the United States of America, and from 1880 there was mass emigration from Russia and other Eastern European countries to the New World. In 1880 the Jewish population of the United States stood at approximately a quarter of a million and between 1881 and 1914 approximately two million more Jews emigrated to America. The newcomers initially crowded into the big cities, where they worked in small factories and unhealthy sweatshops. The Eastern European Jews brought with them all their strictly Orthodox customs and practices, and many of the assimilated German-Jews who were already settled in the country found them disconcerting: they were too Jewish. None-the-less, they rallied to help their coreligionists and the Jewish Theological Seminary was founded in New York to train more Orthodox rabbis than was done at the established reform seminary in Cincinnati. The American Jewish Committee was set up to lobby the government on Jewish issues abroad, and the Anti-Defamation League was organized to counter anti-Semitism at home. The Hebrew Immigrant Aid Society helped the newcomers settle in their new homes, and a host of other Jewish charities were also created.

The new immigrants quickly learned American ways. They were anxious that their children should speak English rather than Yiddish, and they wanted the best possible education for them. Within a generation the old distinction between the established German-Jews and the new Russian-Jews had largely disappeared: they had all become Americans.

ABOVE: Jewish Immigration

The Zionist Dream

Not all Jewish emigrants from Europe chose the United States. Between 1881 and 1914 350,000 settled in Western Europe, 200,000 in Great Britain, 40,000 in South Africa, 115,000 in Argentina, and 100,000 in Canada. When World War I broke out in 1914, the map of the Jewish world was very different to that of 50 years previously. No longer were the

majority of Jews living their enclosed lives in the old Jewish villages of Eastern Europe; there was now an attainable alternative. Also things had changed at home. Inevitably, as individuals emigrated, they wrote back to their families and friends about the freedoms inherent in their new lives. Gradually – even in the villages – the old customs and disciplines which had kept the communities together, began to break down. Increasingly, however, the idea of a new and different homeland began to take hold – a land in which the majority of citizens would be Jews, a land in which Jews would no longer be guests of an unsympathetic host nation.

The old dream of returning to the Promised Land had always been retained in the Jewish community. Indeed, it was an integral part of the liturgy: during prayer, the Jew faces toward Jerusalem' he prays for rain according to the needs of the land of Israel, and three times a day he begs the Almighty for a return of the Exiles to Zion. When he says grace after his meals, he asks God to "rebuild Jerusalem, the Holy City, speedily in our days," and when leaving a house of mourning, he traditionally says, "May the Almighty console you among the mourners of Zion and Jerusalem." Most poignantly of all, at the end of the annual Passover service, the leader says "Next year in Jerusalem!" Traditionally the hope of a return was connected with the coming of the Messiah. The long-promised king would gather together the scattered tribes of Israel from the ends of the earth; when all were gathered in, then all the nations of the world would turn to Jerusalem to learn about the One God.

Through the centuries there was a constant trickle of Jews who did return to the homeland. After the great expulsion of Jews from Spain at the end of the 15th century, groups of refugees settled there and established the great mystical center of Safed. Later, groups of Hasidim and Mitnagdim traveled to the holy cities – very often in order to be buried in the sacred soil. Then, after the 1881 pogroms, several thousand Russian-Jews left for Palestine, earning their livings there as artisans or shopkeepers. Other immigrants, often inspired by strong socialist convictions, went out to work the land and established farming settlements. Throughout Russia, Poland and Romania, *Hibbat Zion* [Love of Zion] societies were set up, with the aim of raising money to buy further land for settlement.

During this period, a highly influential pamphlet was published by Leon Pinsker (1821-91), a Russian doctor. In *Autoemancipation* he argued that Jewish freedom could only be ensured by the establishment of a Jewish state, for in any country where Jews were in a minority, they were in danger of anti-Semitic persecution. Emigration to the New World was no solution as Jews would still only form a small proportion of the total population. Peace between the nations was dependent on at least token equality between them, but living in exile, the Jews could never attain that equality. *Autoemancipation* was widely read and discussed throughout Eastern Europe. The founder of modern political Zionism, however, is generally reckoned to be Theodor Herzl (1860-1904).

Herzl worked as a journalist in Vienna, the capital of the Austro-Hungarian Empire. As a secularly educated Jew, he had initially believed that the problem of anti-Semitism would be solved by assimilation into the

הרצל

majority culture. However, he was present at the Dreyfus trial, and the sound of the crowd outside baying for Jewish blood haunted him. He realized that Jews would always face difficulties while they remained in a minority situation. In 1896 he published his work *Der Judenstaat* (The Jewish State), in which he suggested that it would be to everyone's advantage if a Jewish state were to be founded by international agreement, and believed that the Holy Land would obviously be the most desirable location for the new state. Herzl did not persuade everyone: the assimilationists still thought anti-Semitism would disappear if only Jews were perceived to be good citizens of their host countries. In the Pittsburgh Platform of 1885 the Reform movement had insisted that "We consider ourselves no longer a nation, but a religious community, and expect neither a return to Palestine . . . nor the restoration of any of the laws concerning the Jewish state." On the other extreme wing, the strictly Orthodox Jews believed that such a return would only come about with the arrival of the Messiah; they were unequivocal in their condemnation of Herzl's premature anticipation of God's plan.

Nonetheless, many young Jews were inspired by Herzl, and the *Hibbat Zion* supported him. In 1897 he convened the First Zionist Conference, which took place in Basel and was chaired by Herzl himself. The conferences became annual events, and Herzl threw himself into building up international support. He himself was willing to consider other places besides Palestine as a possible Jewish homeland: at various stages a tract of Turkey, Cyprus, the Sinai Peninsula and an area in Uganda were considered. This last was a real possibility, since the British gave it their support. After seeing the miserable condition of the Jews in the Russian Pale of Settlement, Herzl reluctantly agreed to the Ugandan plan, but it caused an uproar at the Sixth Zionist Conference, and in 1904 Herzl was compelled to reaffirm his commitment to Palestine at a plenary session of the

FAR LEFT AND ABOVE:The tomb and birthplace plaque of the founder of modern political Zionism: Theodor Herzl (1860-1904).

Zionism

Zionist Action Committee. He died later that year, at the early age of 43; the strain of the negotiations had almost certainly contributed to the breakdown of his health. Many years later, after the state of Israel had been founded, his body was disinterred and reburied in Jerusalem.

The Zionist movement quickly split into factions. Many Orthodox Jews did become Zionists, but they were determined to preserve strictly Orthodox ways within the Jewish state; to this end they founded the Mizrachi party in 1902. On the other hand, Jews who were committed socialists joined the *Poale Zion* (the Labor Zionist party), which saw the Jewish state as a potential showcase for their own political theories. Some Jews wanted the emphasis to be on purchase of land and practical work in Palestine, while others saw political negotiation as being the only way forward. As a result of these conflicts, the second president of the World Zionist Organization, David Wolffson (1856-1914) failed to be re-elected to the presidency in 1911.

Meanwhile, within Palestine itself there was increased Jewish immigration. The Palestine Jewish Colonization Association encouraged the newcomers to work in farming communities, but there were also sizable groups in the cities. Then, after the second wave of Russian pogroms in 1904, large numbers of Jews left for the Promised Land, and most of these, influenced by Poale Zion, were committed to earning their living on the land. Prominent among this group was David Gordon (1856-1922), who insisted that for "too long have the hands been the hands of Esau and the voice the voice of Jacob. It is time for Jacob to use his hands too!" The young David Ben-Gurion (1886-1973), later the first prime minister of the new Jewish state after World War II, was also one of these immigrants.

It is notable that many early Zionists were non-religious; Herzl himself had justified the creation of a new state not on religious, but on political grounds. It was to be a refuge from anti-Semitism, not in any sense a theocracy. Some early writers, such as Judah Alkali (1798-1878) and Tzevi Hirsch Kalischer (1795-1874) had attempted to justify the return to Zion for religious reasons, but they were in the minority. Indeed, many of the strictly Orthodox felt that such a move was blasphemy, a premature anticipation of God's plans, and that only the long-promised Messiah could lead his people back in triumph to Jerusalem. The Mizrachi party was specifically created to counter the antireligious stance of the secular Zionists; its motto was "The Land of Israel to the people of Israel according to the Law of Israel." The co-operation between the *Mizrachi* and the secular Zionists, however, caused much offense and was condemned by many leading rabbis of the time and, particularly among the Hasidim, the mood was hostile.

The Mizrachi and the World Zionist Organization fell out on the question of education. Traditionally in the Jewish world, education was under the control of the religious authorities, but in 1911 the Tenth Zionist Conference passed a motion making itself responsible for the educational activities of the movement. Many members of the Mizrachi promptly disassociated themselves from this, founding the *Agudat Israel,* which opposed

BELOW: David Ben-Gurion (1886-1973), later the first prime minister of the new Jewish state after World War II, was an early immigrant to Palestine.

any form of political Zionism, and instead pursued a policy of complete noncooperation with the secular Zionists. Branches were formed in all the leading Jewish centers in Europe to support the traditional institutions of Orthodox-Jewish learning. Later, socialist groups, known as the *Poel Mizrachi* and the *Poel Agudat* Israel, emerge from both the Mizrachi and the Agudat Israel. Since the foundation of the state of Israel in 1948, all four religious parties have put forward candidates for election.

From the earliest days of the Zionist movement there was a determination to create a Hebrew rather than a Yiddish culture, and children were taught in Hebrew schools and were encouraged to use Hebrew in their day-to-day speech. Ben Yehuda (1858-1922), a philologist, compiled the first dictionary of modern Hebrew, and there was a conscious attempt to create a new Hebrew literature; prominent early writers included Ahad Ha-Am (1856-1927), Reubin Brainin (1862-1939) and Chaim Nachman Bialik (1873-1934). Ahad Ha-Am, in particular, believed that the essence of Jewishness lay not in the Jewish religion, but in the Jewish experience. He insisted that the love of Zion "stands for a Judaism which shall have as its focal point the ideal of our nation's unity, its renaissance and its free development through the expression of universal human values in terms of its own distinctive spirit." On the other hand, the socialists continued to work for the establishment of a socialist state in Palestine. Nahman Syrkin (1868-1924), for example, believed that a socialist Israel would simply be a secularized version of the Messianic promise. To this end, the socialists worked for the establishment of model villages and collective settlements such as the *kevutzot* (the forerunners of the *kibbutzim.*)

World War I changed the social order of every country it touched; and as we have already seen, the overthrow of the czar in 1917 and the revolutionary wars which followed resulted in the massacre of whole Jewish communities in Russia. Inevitably, more families decided to emigrate abroad, but in 1921 and 1924 the United States passed restrictive immigration laws; several other Western countries did the same. Meanwhile, the League of Nation had agreed that Britain should administer Palestine. By 1918 the Jewish community in Palestine numbered approximately 90,000 people; it increased steadily throughout the 1920s and 1930s, and was estimated at 160,000 in 1929, and nearly 500,000 10 years later. The Arab population became uneasy at this quickly growing number of Jewish settlers; between the wars, there were about a million Palestinians of Arab origin, and in 1929 there were serious anti-Jewish riots, which prompted the British to cut back on Jewish immigration.

Back in 1917, in order to gain Jewish support during World War I, the British government had issued the Balfour Declaration, which promised support for the establishment of a national home for the Jewish people in Palestine. In 1937, however, in view of the poor relationships between the Palestinian Arabs and the Jewish settlers, a British royal commission advocated that the land be divided between the two groups; even this policy was subsequently rejected in a 1939 white paper which limited Jewish immigration still further. While these negotiations were taking place, the German Nazi party was growing in power – pledged to the destruction of

FAR RIGHT: Nahalal was one of the early co-operative villages built in Palestine in 1921.

ABOVE and RIGHT: Deganya A was one of the first of the collective settlements which would become known as the kibbutzim. It was the scene of fierce fighting in the 1948 War of Independence.

CHAPTER NINE

HOLOCAUST

Anti-Semitism Between the Wars

After the carnage of World War I, Jews became the scapegoats for all the problems facing German society. Oswald Spengler, in his work *The Decline of the West*, argued that there was inevitable misunderstanding between the "Faustian" nations (in particular Germany) and the "Magian" nations (pre-eminently the Jews): "The belief in the inevitability of this misunderstanding," he wrote, "leads finally to a frightening hatred, deeply concentrated in the blood, attaching itself to symbolic signs such as race, lifestyle, profession, language, which leads both sides to bloody explosions."

Such feelings were not confined to Germany: this was the era of the most terrible pogroms in Russia, and the years in which the *Protocols of the Elders of Zion* were most freely circulated. In Britain, anti-Semitic attitudes became commonplace. Rudyard Kipling, the most popular author and poet of his time, wrote his poem *Gehazi* with the intention of illustrating the dishonest guile of Jewish politicians: "Stand up, stand up Gehazi / Draw close thy robe and go / Gehazi, Judge in Israel / A leper white as snow!" In 1902 the Bishop of Stepney had compared the influx of Jewish refugees from Russia to a conquering army who "eat the Christians out of house and home." The British Union of Fascists, led by Sir Oswald Mosley, was avowedly anti-Jewish and attracted many members, even from the educated classes: Jessica Mitford, in her autobiographical book *Hons and Rebels* records how her sisters Unity and Diana became involved, how Unity became a personal friend of Hitler, and how Diana married Mosley. The widely read detective stories of Agatha Christie and Dorothy L. Sayers contain several unflattering references to "Jewboys" of doubtful integrity.

In the United States, it was commonly supposed that the Bolshevik revolution in Russia had been stirred up by the Jews. The British essayist Hilaire Belloc described the situation after a visit to New York: "The Jews are barely admitted to the Jewish country clubs and most of them are barred. Their talents are rarely used on the general staff of the army. They have no real civic standing. They are excluded from I don't know how many hotels." The industrialist Henry Ford was convinced that there was a Jewish plot to take over the world, while one of the stated aims of the Ku Klux Klan was to prevent the Jews from gaining a foothold on mainstream American life.

The anti-Semitic attitudes of these inter-war years crystallized into Adolf

Hitler's conviction that the Jewish people were an evil race bent on world domination. Hitler explained his position in his book *Mein Kampf* (My Struggle), as well as in his speeches. His revulsion comes through clearly:

"With satanic joy on his face, the black-haired Jewish youth lurks in wait for the unsuspecting girl whom he defiles with his blood, thus stealing her from her people. With every means he tries to destroy the racial foundations of the people he sets out to subjugate. Just as he systematically ruins women and girls, he does not shrink back from pulling down the blood barriers of others, even on a large scale. It was and it is Jews who bring the Negroes into the Rhineland, always with the same secret and clear aim of ruining the hated white race by the necessarily resulting bastardization, throwing it down from its cultural and political height and himself rising to be its master."

Hitler's Nazi party was a comparatively minor force in Germany throughout the 1920s; in November 1923 it had attempted a coup in Munich that had failed. But the Great Depression, triggered by the Wall Street crash of 1929, was Hitler's chance. There was massive inflation; the industrialists feared a communist takeover; the lower-middle classes were insecure about their social position, and the young were attracted to Hitler's certainties. In 1928 the Nazi party won little more than 800,000 votes in the elections; in 1930 that figure had increased to more than six million, and in 1932 to 14 million. Then, on March 5, 1933, the Nazis gained 44 percent of the total vote, and Hitler was invited by the aged Marshal Paul von Hindenburg to be Chancellor of Germany.

Hitler immediately consolidated his position: in the spring and summer of 1933 all other political parties were outlawed; strikes were forbidden and trade unions were dismantled. As early as March 1933, public book-burn-

BELOW: Hitler is greeted by von Hindenburg in February 1934. He would become President and Chancellor on von Hindenburg's death in August 1934 and begin the inexorable slide toward the Holocaust.

ings were taking place, and several left-wing artists and writers were imprisoned. In June 1934, the Nazi party's social radicals were eliminated in a purge and, under their leader Heinrich Himmler, the Nazi S.S. took over many of the functions of the civilian police. After Hindenburg's death in 1934, Hitler became head of the German state.

Hitler was now secure enough to begin his campaign of Jewish persecution. In 1935 all sexual relationships between Jews and non-Jews were forbidden as crimes against the state. Then, in 1938, all the communal bodies of the Jews were put under the direct control of the Gestapo, the Nazi secret police, and every Jewish citizen was forced to register their property. In the same year the Nazi party organized a concerted attack against the Jewish population: in a single night, *Kristallnacht* (the Night of Glass), Jewish businesses and shops were destroyed; synagogues were burned to the ground and a number of Jewish citizens were murdered. The destruction was not just the work of Nazi storm-troopers: many ordinary citizens joined in with enthusiasm. According to observers in the village of Hoengen, "The storm-troopers were joined by people who were not in uniform; and suddenly with one loud cry of 'Down with the Jews!', the gathering outside produced axes and heavy sledge hammers . . . soon the little synagogue was but a heap of stone, broken glass and smashed up woodwork . . ."

Many German Jews realized the gravity of the situation and frantically tried to emigrate. It was not easy: there was restriction on Jewish immigration to Palestine; while because of the Depression, the United States government was accepting very few new citizens. The situation was the same throughout Western Europe. Desperate families did what they could: children were entrusted to friends and business associates overseas; some looked as far afield as South Africa or South America for refuge. All too many, however, had no choice: they had to stay.

The Destruction of European Jewry

The first stage of the Nazis' plan for the destruction of European Jewry began with the invasion of Poland in September 1939; the Allies were committed to the defense of Poland, so the invasion led to a formal declaration of war. From then on travel became difficult, and Jewish emigration from Nazi-occupied territory nearly impossible. In every conquered Polish town the Jews were subject to special attention: they were forced to hand over their valuables, to clean the streets, to clear rubble, to carry heavy loads and to clean latrines with their prayer shawls or their bare hands. The soldiers delighted in humiliating them, cutting off their beards and side-curls and laughing at their discomfort.

A massive work program was now instituted. The condition of the work camps has been described by many eyewitnesses, and their accounts make horrifying reading. The following is a record of a mass slaughter of Jews at a camp during the spring of 1940.

"All the Jews were assembled in the courtyard; they were ordered to run, to drop down and to stand up again. Anybody who was slow in obeying the order was beaten to death by the overseer with the butt of his rifle.

Images of the Holocaust.
FAR LEFT: The little Insurgents Monument in Warsaw commemorating the children killed in the 1944 uprising,

LEFT: Railway tracks lead to the entrance of the Auschwitz-Birkenau death camp.

BELOW: Monument in Warsaw marking the loading point for trains for Treblinka.

Afterwards Jews were ordered to jump right into the cesspit of the latrines which were being built; this was full of urine. The taller Jews got out again since the level reached their chin, but the shorter ones went down. The young ones tried to help the old folk and, as a punishment, the overseers ordered the latter to beat the young. When they refused to obey, they were cruelly beaten themselves."

With the invasion of Russia in 1941, the next stage in the plan for exterminating the Jews began. Battalions of between 500 and 900 men were formed known as *Einsatzgruppen*; their mission was the slaughter of Russian Jewry. Throughout the occupied territories, the *Einsatzgruppen* moved into the towns, sought out the local rabbi or Jewish council and demanded a list of all the Jewish inhabitants. Then the Jews were systematically rounded up in a central place, crammed into trains, buses or trucks and taken to the woods outside the town where mass graves had already been dug. The people were lined up and machine-gunned so that they fell down into the pits. Another eyewitness describes the scene thus:

LEFT: Nazi anti-Semitic propaganda pre-World War II.

Map depicting the consentration camps and death camps in Europe

"People were closely wedged together, lying on top of each other so that only their heads were visible. Nearly all had blood running over their shoulders from heads. Some of the people shot were still moving. Some lifted their arms and turned their heads to show they were still alive. The pit was already two-thirds full. I estimated that it held a thousand people."

In the first sweep through occupied Russia, these troops are thought to have killed over 300,000 Jews. In the second stage, which lasted throughout 1942, another 900,000 were slaughtered.

However, the German leaders considered this method of destroying the Jews of Europe too slow and unreliable. From 1941, therefore, experiments began to be conducted using poison gas. In the beginning, the *Einsatzgruppen* were sent mobile gas units; the Jews were pushed into the enclosed cars, the cars began to move, the gas was released and, after a short journey, all the Jews were dead and their bodies could be buried in the waiting pits. But again this procedure was felt to be insufficiently systematic. On January 20, 1942, Reinhard Heydrich, the deputy commander of the Gestapo, announced Hitler's "Final Solution" to the Jewish problem at a conference in Wannsee in Berlin. The plan was that the Jews would be deported to special camps in the east; those who were capable of working for the benefit of the Third Reich would be worked until they could be worked no more. The rest would be exterminated on arrival.

The plan was carried out with ruthless efficiency. By 1942 the Nazis were in control of most of Europe: from Norway, Denmark, the Netherlands, France, Germany, Italy, Austria, Serbia, Croatia, Bulgaria, Albania, Rumania, Hungary, Bohemia, Slovakia, Lithuania, Latvia, Estonia, Poland, to Ukraine and occupied Russia, the Jews were isolated, crammed together, and then transported – often in cattle trucks – to the new camps.

Five special "death camps" were set up in remote areas of Poland, namely Chelmno, Belzec, Majdanek, Sobibor and Treblinka. Most notorious of all was Auschwitz, which was situated near Crackow in Poland; here there were gas chambers which could destroy 12,000 individuals every day. On arrival the young and fit were selected for work – indeed the gates of Auschwitz bore the legend *Arbeit macht frei* (Work makes free) – and they were sent to the nearby slave-labor camps. As they became worn down by starvation, ill-treatment and exhaustion, they were "selected" to return to the main camp to join the old, the children and the infirm in the gas chambers. The eminent scientist and writer Primo Levi was a prisoner in Auschwitz and vividly describes his experiences in his book *If This is a Man*. The figures speak for themselves: the camp was the central extermination center for Western Europe and, at its greatest capacity, could hold 140,000 inmates. There were five crematoria working at full capacity to dispose of the bodies of those who died in the gas chambers. Altogether, it has been estimated that approximately two million Jews died in Auschwitz, together with unspecified numbers of gypsies, homosexuals and others regarded as "subhuman" by the Nazi state.

This was not the end of the horrors. There were other camps which were not specifically extermination centres, which also systematically worked Jews and others to death. When the Allied forces finally liberated occupied

Europe from the Nazi regime, they could not believe the degradation that they uncovered. In Buchenwald, for example, they found 21,000 starving, barely human, survivors, thousands of unburied corpses and the ashes of many more. In addition, there were warehouses full of personal possessions, wedding rings, human hair, spectacles and articles of clothing. It was also clear that pseudoscientific experiments had been conducted on live human subjects. All these scenes were filmed and shown on newsreels to a horrified world.

Resistance

As the murder of the Jews continued, resistance spread. In September 1942, the Jews of Korzec in Russia set alight the walls of the ghetto into which they had been herded. In the same month, in the Polish town of Kaluszyn, the chairman of the Jewish council tried to prevent the deportation of his people by collecting money; he hoped to ransom those Jews already assembled in the main square. When he realized that, despite all his efforts, the transports were to take place anyway, he tore the money into small pieces and hit the German overseer in the face, calling him a bloody tyrant. He was immediately shot by the Ukrainian guards. There were several other breakouts from prison camps and ghettos, and many of the fugitives formed small partisan groups.

The most famous rebellion against the Nazis took place in the Warsaw ghetto. A small area of the city had been walled off, and the entire Jewish population of Warsaw and its surrounding area had been crammed into the quarter's old buildings. As the population became decimated by starvation, overwork and deportation, the Jewish "Fighting Organization" prepared itself for action. As an eyewitness described it:

BELOW: Resistance commemorated in Warsaw's monument to the heroes of the ghetto.

"The community wants the enemy to pay dearly. They will attack them with knives, sticks, carbolic acid; they will not allow themselves to be seized in the street, because now they know that labor camps these days mean death."

On January 18, 1943, German troops entered the ghetto to carry out further deportations. They were not expecting any trouble, but, unknown to them, preparations had been made for months: pistols and hand grenades had been smuggled in from the "Aryan" side; homemade bombs and explosives had been manufactured in the tenements; for those who had nothing else, there were sticks, bottles and lengths of piping. As the people began to be rounded up, a small group began to throw grenades at the soldiers. The scene was described vividly:

"The fighters set up a barricade in a little house on Nivska Street and held it against German reinforcements which soon arrived. The Germans found it impossible to enter the house, so they set it afire. The fighters inside continued firing until the last bullet . . . though the unit was destroyed, the battle of Nivska Street encouraged us. For the first time since the occupation, we saw Germans clinging to the walls, crawling on the ground, running for cover, hesitating before making a step in fear of being hit by a bullet. The cries of the wounded caused us joy, and increased our thirst for battle."

Several months later, the Jews learned that the Germans intended to destroy the ghetto completely. The commander of the Jewish resistance group, Mordecai Anilewicz, declared, "He who has arms will fight!" The Germans entered the ghetto on April 19, 1943, and the fighters were ready for them. As one of the survivors described, "When the Germans came near to our posts and marched by us, we threw those hand grenades and bombs and saw blood pouring over the streets of Warsaw." The Germans systematically shelled the buildings, and by the beginning of May only 120 fighters remained in an underground bunker. The Germans bombarded the entrance for two hours and used gas to try to flush the Jews out. A few managed to escape by a secret entrance, but, like the Jewish rebels at Masada, many in the Warsaw ghetto chose to commit suicide rather than fall into the hands of the enemy.

Even in the camps there was resistance. At a labor camp in Kruszyna, the Jews turned against their captors with knives and fists. At the Kopernik camp near Minsk, the Jews barricaded themselves into a building and resisted with sticks, stones and bricks. In the death camp of Sobibor in October 1943, there was a mass breakout; although 150 inmates were captured, at least an equal number escaped. Similarly, at Auschwitz prisoners managed to blow up two of the crematoria.

Despite their awful plight, the Jewish fasts and festivals were observed in the camps; one of the participants described the Day of Atonement at Birkenau:

"The oppressive silence was broken by a mournful tune. It was the plaintive tones of the ancient *Kol Nidre* ['All our vows'] prayer . . . when at last he was silent, there was exaltation among us, an exaltation which men can experience only when they have fallen as low as we have fallen and then, through the mystic power of a deathless prayer, have awaken ed once more to the world of the spirit."

There were a few attempts by gentiles to help the Jews. The Danes organized a secret flotilla of small boats to evacuate its Jewish population to neutral Sweden. The resistance movements within the occupied countries did their best to provide safe houses; Jews were even hidden in Hitler's capital city, Berlin. Anne Frank, the author of the famous diary, and her family were concealed by non-Jewish friends in a house in Amsterdam. The Swedish diplomat Raoul Wallenberg issued thousands of Hungarian Jews with false identity and travel documents so they could settle in neutral countries; he was imprisoned by the Soviet government after the war and was never heard from again. The industrialist Oskar Schindler protected the Jews who worked in his factory near Cracow in Poland.

Despite these examples of help, too many Christians turned their backs on the sufferings of the Jews. For example, when asked by the Vichy government in France about the legitimacy of the anti-Semitic legislation imposed by the Nazis, the Vatican declared: "In principle there is nothing in these measures which the Holy See would find to criticize." Again, when the pope was asked whether he would protest against the persecution of the Jews, he replied, "Dear friend, do not forget that millions of Catholics serve in the German armies. Shall I bring them into conflicts of conscience?"

By the end of the war, it is estimated that the Nazis had killed six million Jews. The old synagogues, Talmudic academies, and places of Jewish learning had been destroyed forever. The life of the shtetl had gone from Europe and European Jewry had been decimated.

Jewish Thought after the Holocaust

The deaths of six million European Jews have raised an enormous religious problem for the Jewish community. The foundation of Israel's faith is liberation. According to the sacred Book of Exodus, the Jews were oppressed and enslaved in Egypt and endured hideous treatment from their Egyptian taskmasters. Yet their God, the God of their ancestors, took the initiative and saved them from captivity. After visiting 10 dreadful plagues upon the Land of Egypt, He led them out of the country; He drowned their pursuing enemy in the Red Sea; He guided them through the wilderness by means of a pillar of a cloud; He fed them on manna and quail in the desert; He gave them the laws by which they live. And ultimately He brought them to the land of Israel, the Promised Land, the land flowing with milk and honey where they could live in freedom and dignity.

So where was God during the Holocaust? Why did He sit in silence while a third of His chosen people perished in the squalor of Bergen-Belsen and the gas chambers of Auschwitz? If He was capable of defeating the pharaoh, one of the most powerful kings of the ancient world, surely He could have struck down Hitler. If He loves His people, then their fate in the concentration camps of Eastern Europe must have been intolerable for Him. If we, as human beings, find the story of the Holocaust almost unbearable, how much the worse must it be for a being who is all-loving and all-powerful?

For many, the Holocaust is a confirmation that there is no God. On Christmas Day in 1943, a group of starving Jewish women were brought from the barracks to the extermination center at Birkenau. Trucks drove up to the block and the women were herded into them; they knew that they were destined for the gas chambers, but those who tried to escape were shot down. When they were all inside the trucks and the engines started up, a terrible noise arose: the death cry of thousands of young women. One of the observers was the son of a rabbi. He prayed, "God, show them Your power. They are acting against You." Nothing happened and, in despair, the boy cried out, "There is no God!"

Some theologians have echoed this view. Richard Rubenstein, in his book *After Auschwitz*, argues that the Nazi death camps were a decisive refutation of the traditional Jewish belief that God cares for the fate of His people. It is no longer possible to believe that God has chosen the Jews, or that

He intervenes in the course of history. Instead of clinging blindly to the old faith, it is better to return to the values of ancient Canaanite paganism and affirm the values of human life as part of the natural order. Finally, the God of the Jews must be seen as the "Ultimate Nothing." Rubenstein has been reviled by the religious establishment for his view, but the fact remains that for many Jews the Holocaust is the final proof that there is no God. Rather than face the possibility of an impotent God who is unable to prevent the horrors of Auschwitz, or a wicked God who does not even want to prevent innocent suffering, it is easier to abandon the whole enterprise. Such Jews identity with the community only through their common ethnic background, and by maintaining financial support for Jewish charities and institutions.

Others have taken a different line. Ignaz Maybaum, a British non-Orthodox rabbi, has argued in his work *The Face of God after Auschwitz* that the Jews who died in a death camps were chosen by God to become sacrificial victims. By their deaths, like the suffering servant in the Book of Isaiah, they suffered vicariously for the sins of humanity. He believed that Auschwitz was the 20th-century calvary of the Jewish people, and that the cross had been replaced by the gas chamber. As a result of the Holocaust, human beings have looked into the abyss, and they must realize that the only hope for the future lies in greater compassion to one another. By perceiving Auschwitz as a new exodus from the past into the future, it is God's plan that justice, kindness and peace can be established in the world.

At the other end of the religious spectrum, the Orthodox thinker Bernard Maza argued that the purpose of the Holocaust was to bring Jews back into the fold of Orthodox Judaism. In the 20th century, the life of the shtetl, the Jewish village, was breaking down through the forces of secularism; the Jewish people seemed to be on the road to self-extinction. The Holocaust was the pouring out of God's wrath. The righteous martyrs in the concentration camps proclaimed their trust in the will of God and, by means of their suffering, the Jewish people were brought back to their senses. Particularly in Israel, but also in the United States, there has been a resurgence of Torah Judaism after the war; strictly Orthodox Jewish life has flourished again.

Emil Fackenheim struck a chord in the Jewish community by arguing that the Holocaust was an expression of God's will that his chosen people must survive. Through the concentration camps, God has issued his 614th Commandment, "You shall not grant Hitler a posthumous victory." For the sake of Jewish survival, denial or despair of God is forbidden. Then the Orthodox thinker, Eliezer Berkovitz, argued in *Faith after the Holocaust* that there is no rational explanation for the death camps and that Jews can only keep their faith in an ever silent God whose activities are hidden from human understanding. He has expressed the hope that "Perhaps in the awful misery of man will be revealed to us the awesome mystery of God." For many Jews, however, the focus of their interest has switched from religion to politics. It is in the creation of the state of Israel that Jews have found their new focus. Indeed, the only contact many Jews today have with their coreligionists is in their support for the new state of Israel.

The Foundation of the State of Israel

At the end of World War II, six million European Jews were dead – a direct result of the old legacy of Christian anti-Semitism. World Jewry was aghast: German Jews had been perceived as the most educated and assimilated of all the Jewish communities, but it was the German government which had sent the Jews of Europe to the crematoria of the death camps. There was an immediate world-wide shift of opinion to the Zionist cause, for it seemed that Jews could only be safe in their own country. Even the leaders of Reform congregations, who were traditionally committed to the idea of being a full citizen of the host country, were persuaded: the Zionist cause had come into its own.

Once the full horror of the concentration camps had been revealed, even moderate Zionists were caught up in the fever of the campaign. All over Europe the survivors were living in miserable conditions in displaced persons' camps. Many of those who had tried to go back to their old homes found they were not welcome: their gentile neighbors had taken over their property and were not prepared to return it. For others Europe held too many evil memories: in its towns and villages their families and friends had been tortured and murdered – it could no longer be home. It was clear that something had to be done for these people.

Despite the Jewish support for the Allied cause throughout the war, there was serious Jewish opposition to British policy in Palestine. According to the 1939 British white paper, Jewish immigration was to be severely limited; as a result Palestine was no refuge for Jews during the war. Illegal landings were prevented, and there were several ugly incidents. In 1942, for example, a Rumanian ship, the *Struma*, laden with Jewish refugees, was refused permission to land; on its journey back to Rumania, it sank in the Black Sea with the loss of nearly 800 lives. Meanwhile, the Jews of Palestine were forming their own lines of defense. The Union of Zionist Revisionists was determined to work single-mindedly for the establishment of an independent Jewish state. Even before the war, it had withdrawn its members from the permitted Jewish militia and formed its own group, the Irgun. In 1943 Menahem Begin (1913-92) took over as its leader, determined to use his own tactics to force the British to withdraw. On November 6, 1944, for example, an extremist group – the Stern Gang – assassinated Lord Moyne, the British minister for middle-eastern affairs.

After the war, a united Jewish resistance movement was created in Palestine. The Irgun continued its campaign of terror, and its cause was forcibly brought to the attention of the world with the bombing of the King David Hotel in Jerusalem. Although Chaim Weizman (1874-1952), the president of the World Zionist Organization, distanced himself from these activities, the Irgun proceeded to hang two British sergeants in retaliation for the hanging of three Jewish terrorists. The British felt that they could no longer cope with the situation and handed over responsibility for Palestine to the newly formed United Nations.

In May 1947 the whole question of Palestine and a Jewish state came up for discussion in the assembly, during which President Harry S. Truman of

ABOVE: The Yad Vashem memorial to the Holocaust is a moving tribute to the six million Jews who perished during World War II.

the United States threw his weight behind the Zionist cause. There is no doubt that he was personally sympathetic, but he was also anxious to secure the Jewish vote in the 1948 presidential elections. Despite violent opposition from the Arab nations, on November 29, 1947 it was formally agreed that Palestine should be partitioned into a Jewish and an Arab state, and that the city of Jerusalem should be an international zone. The world now waited for the inevitable Arab reaction; the new Jewish state was surrounded by hostile nations – Palestine, Egypt, Syria, Iraq and Lebanon. The Jews were outnumbered, and it was confidently expected that they would be driven back into the sea by the Arabs.

Events did not turn out like that, however. The Palestinians began to attack Jewish settlements, but, under the leadership of David Ben-Gurion (1886-1973), the Jews consolidated their position. They occupied Haifa, opened the route between Tiberias and Eastern Galilee and captured the towns of Safed, Jaffa and Acre. On May 14, 1948, Ben-Gurion formally declared the independence of the Jewish state in Palestine, to be known in the future as the State of Israel. The claim was based on "national and intrinsic right," as well as on the international resolution passed by the United Nations.

The War of Independence, as it was called, continued throughout 1948, and by 1949 the Israelis were in possession of large tracts of land beyond boundaries designated by the United Nations. An armistice was eventually signed between Israel and Egypt, Lebanon, Syria and Jordan, agreeing that the Jews would have their own state, and that Jerusalem was to be partitioned between Israel and Jordan. The peace was not permanent, however; Israel felt itself to be perpetually under siege, and war broke out again in 1954, 1967 (when the Israeli's captured the Arab portion of Jerusalem) and 1973. An enormous proportion of the Israeli gross national product had to be spent on defense; young women as well as young men

were subject to military service, and there was the ongoing problem of refugees. During the War of Independence more than half a million Palestinian Arabs had fled from their homes to escape the Israeli army. Some were taken in by surrounding countries, but too many were compelled to live in squalor in makeshift refugee camps, to be a constant source of discontent, ferment and guerrilla activity.

In the meantime, there was a flood of new immigrants into Israel, both victims of the Holocaust and Jews who lived in the surrounding Arab countries. As a result, a completely new infrastructure had to be created; houses, schools, colleges, hospitals and clinics had to be built. The new country was very dependent on international aid, and now world Jewry found a cause and a focus. Today, Jews everywhere view the white Israeli flag, with its blue Star of David, with enormous pride; however loyal they may remain to their host country, they nonetheless have a stake in the state of Israel. Jews are no longer a people in exile, a people with no country of their own: in a very real sense, Israel is the nation for all Jews.

CHAPTER TEN

THE JEWISH COMMUNITY TODAY

The State of Israel

The Holocaust and the founding of the state of Israel completely changed the population distribution of world Jewry. Before 1939, there were approximately nine million Jews living in Europe; by 1945 there were only three million. Altogether there are probably approximately 14 million Jews alive in the world today. The United States has the largest community, with approximately five-and-three-quarter million, while nearly three-quarters of a million live in Canada, Mexico and South America. Israel has a Jewish population of about three-and-a-half million. After the creation of the new state, all limitations on Jewish immigration were lifted, except in the case of the chronically sick.

According to the Israeli Law of Return, any Jew anywhere in the world may go to their local Israeli embassy and register as an Israeli citizen. Israel is truly a state for the Jewish people; never again will Jews facing anti-Semitism find all doors closed to them. Inevitably, however, the vexed question of "Who is a Jew?" has come to the fore. The Orthodox religious parties would like the law to specify that only those born of a Jewish mother or those who have undergone Orthodox conversion qualify. So far this motion has been resisted, and the people who have converted to Judaism under the auspices of the Reform movement are eligible. However the Orthodox do have complete control of jurisdiction in the Israeli courts on matters of personal status; this means that they do not accept Reform converts, or the children of female Reform converts as Jews, and therefore these people cannot get married in Israel. There have been various attempts to introduce forms of civil marriage, but so far these have been unsuccessful. In fact, the vast majority of Israeli citizens are not particularly Orthodox in their practices, but because of the electoral system of proportional representation, the Orthodox political parties have more influence than their numerical strength warrants.

Since 1948 Israel has frequently been under a state of siege. However, in 1978, a historic meeting took place between President Anwar Sadat of Egypt and Menahem Begin. (Although Begin first rose to public notice as leader of the Irgun and was involved in terrorist activities before independence, he was subsequently elected leader of the Likud party and, as such, became prime minister in 1977.) With the meeting of Sadat and Begin, the world hoped that peace would come to the Middle East. It was not so easy,

LEFT: After World War II, Jews flocked to Palestine and the spirit of Masada was rekindled. Four major conflicts ensued during which the Israeli armed forces earned a reputation for skill and efficiency with a people's army. This picture was taken during the great counter-offensive which led to the end of the Yom Kippur War in 1973, when Israeli forces crossed the Suez Canal and encircled the Egyptian Sixth Army.

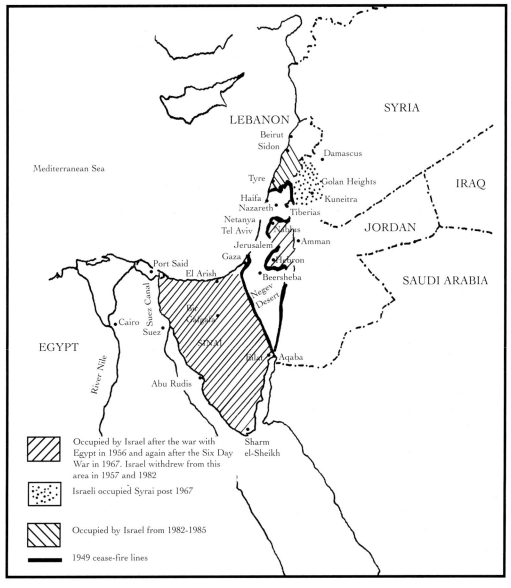

Map showing occupation of Aras land Past-1949.

SYRIA

LEBANON
Beirut
Sidon
Damascus

Mediterranean Sea

Tyre
Golan Heights
Kuneitra
IRAQ

Haifa
Nazareth
Tiberias

Netanya
Tel Aviv
Nablus
JORDAN

Jerusalem
Amman
Gaza
Hebron

Port Said
El Arish
Beersheba

Negev Desert

Suez Canal

Bir Gafgafa

Cairo

Suez
SINAI

Aqaba
Eilat

EGYPT

River Nile

Abu Rudis

SAUDI ARABIA

Sharm el-Sheikh

Occupied by Israel after the war with Egypt in 1956 and again after the Six Day War in 1967. Israel withdrew from this area in 1957 and 1982

Israeli occupied Syrai post 1967

Occupied by Israel from 1982-1985

1949 cease-fire lines

however. In 1982 the Israeli forces invaded Lebanon in order to destroy the bases of the Palestinian Liberation Organization; this destabilized the whole area. Then, in 1987, the Palestinians who lived in the territory occupied by the Israelis since 1967 organized a program of resistance known as the *Intifada*. These Palestinians were largely young, well-educated people; they had benefited from formal programs of instruction, but, at the end of them, they found that there were still few employment opportunities. There were riots throughout the occupied territories; subsequently tactics changed to ambushes, small-scale conflicts and selective strikes. It became increasingly clear that the continued occupation of the West Bank would be a problem for the Israelis.

The Israeli invasion of Lebanon in 1982 swayed world public opinion. The Jews were no longer seen as the outnumbered victims of hostile Arabs; instead they had become the aggressor. The Intifada drew attention to conditions on the West Bank and it became generally felt that the Israelis were guilty of brutality, meeting sticks and stones with tear gas and bullets. Even among Israeli citizens, many believed that the only solution was an autonomous Palestinian state.

In 1992 peace talks began again, and in 1995 a pact was signed between Yasir Arafat, the leader of the Palestine Liberation Organization, and Yitzak Rabin, the Israeli prime minister, as a result of which large tracts of land were handed back to Palestinian self-rule. Many in Israel, particularly the Orthodox settlers on the West Bank, were very unhappy with this, and Rabin himself was assassinated by a fanatical Israeli student. Subsequently the right-wing Binyamin Netanyahu was elected in his place. Many observers expected the peace process would lose its momentum, but as yet the lines of communication between the Israelis and the Palestinians are still open.

BELOW: The start of the peace process: Presidents Sadat (Egypt), Carter (US) and Begin (Israel) at the signing of a peace treaty between the two countries brokered by the US.

LEFT: Yasser Arafat and the PLO have been a thorn in Israel's side for decades. The fate of the Palestinians displaced when Gaza and the West Bank were captured in 1967 has led to continual security problems for Israel, only partly alleviated by military action.

BELOW: With the eyes of the world's press on them, young Palestinians hurl rocks and abuse at Israeli soldiers — part of the continuing Intifada.

ABOVE: The need for security and the Palestinians' continued actions led Israel to send the troops into Lebanon in the 1980s. Here an Israeli-designed and manufactured Merkava tank during Operation "Peace in Galilee."

During all this turmoil there was a constant stream of new immigrants into the country. One result of the creation of the state of Israel was increased hostility toward Jews in Arab countries; Israel was both the cause and the solution to the problem. In Iraq in 1920, Jews formed almost three percent of the population; by1958 almost all had emigrated to Israel. In 1949-50 the Jews of Yemen were airlifted to safety in Israel in "Operation Magic Carpet"; the majority of Turkish Jews now live in Israel as does almost the entire Jewish population of Kurdistan.

It was the same story in North Africa: after the great synagogue of Algiers was raided on Christmas Eve in 1960, the Jews realized that it was time to leave. Many settled in France, but some went to Israel. Tunisian independence in 1956 led to mass Jewish emigration; the Jewish community of Libya has almost entirely resettled in Israel, and Egyptian Jewry, particularly harassed after General Nasser seized power, has mostly emigrated. The King of Morocco has repeatedly promised peace and security to his Jewish subjects, and that country still has the largest Jewish population of any Arab state; even so, it is a mere remnant of the vibrant community that existed before 1948.

The black Jews of Ethiopia have also emigrated *en masse* to Israel. Cut off from the mainstream of Jewish life for centuries, their true origin is not known; however, by 1975 the Israeli government had accepted that they qualified as Jews under the Law of Return. By 1984 approximately 8,000 had settled in Israel, and a further 7,000 were airlifted out of Ethiopia in the face of famine and civil war. Many of these new settlers were completely unfamiliar with the practices of first-world countries, and their settlement was complicated. In addition, the Orthodox rabbinate refused fully to accept their Jewish status and, for marriage, insisted on a symbolic reconversion. This requirement has caused enormous offense, and as yet no final compromise has been achieved.

Meanwhile, in Eastern Europe, too many survivors of the Holocaust found little to keep them in their old countries. The Jews of Poland continued to suffer persecution and discrimination even after the full horrors of the Holocaust were revealed; most emigrated to Israel or elsewhere. The rescue of Soviet Jewry has been another major preoccupation: numerically the Jews of the former Soviet Union form the third-largest Jewish community in the world, but there is also a strong tradition of anti-Semitism. During the life span of the U.S.S.R. discriminatory quotas were applied against Jewish candidates for universities and professional schools, and many Jews came to believe that they and their children could lead fuller lives elsewhere. In common with all citizens of the Soviet Union, Jews were not allowed to travel abroad and applying for an exit visa involved significant risk. However, encouraged by their coreligionists in the West, many did demand to leave for Israel, and some were allowed to go. Numbers leaving varied from year to year, but between 1968 and 1986 more than a quarter of a million Jews left the Soviet Union; with *Perestroika*, still more have gone. By no means have all Russian Jews chosen to settle in Israel, but again the new country has had to provide accommodation and other services for huge numbers of people.

Thus the creation of the state of Israel has been a remarkable achievement. Not only has the government had to organize the defense of the country against hostile neighbors, it has also had to organize the mass settlement of large numbers of very disparate groups of people.

Religious Divisions Within the Community

Although the religious establishment within the state of Israel is Orthodox, the vast majority of Israelis do not follow Orthodox-Jewish practices. It is the same story in the United States, whose Jewish community remains the largest such community in the world, but with only a small proportion of members classifying themselves as Orthodox. Indeed, 53 percent of Jews are not affiliated with any synagogue at all; their identification as Jews is derived from their support for the state of Israel, from belonging to a Jewish communal organization or from the desire to be buried in a Jewish cemetery. Of the remaining 47 percent who do belong to a synagogue, the vast majority have chosen a non-Orthodox example. 23 percent of American-Jewish households belong to a Conservative congregation.

The founder of the Conservative movement was Zacharias Frankel, who was head of the Jewish Theological Seminary in Breslau between 1854 and 1877. On the one hand, he felt that the Reform movement was too radical in its rejection of Jewish nationalism and ethnicity and, on the other, he believed that Orthodoxy was too rigid in its insistence on the divine origin of each and every one of the commandments. Frankel advocated a middle way: he believed that Judaism was the outcome of an evolving historical process, and that Jewish law should continue to be observed but that it should be modified to answer the needs of the times. This point of view was taught in the United States in the Jewish Theological Seminary founded in New York in 1886.

The great leader of the Conservative movement in the United States was

Solomon Schechter, who was elected president of the seminary in 1902, and who founded the movement's lay organization, the United Synagogue, in 1913. Under his leadership the seminary became a leading center of Jewish scholarship. He insisted that Judaism was an organic structure which was capable of taking into account the insights of the modern world without losing its essential nature. Thus, over the years, it was agreed within the movement that women could be called up for the reading of the Law, that women could be counted in the quorum that is necessary for public prayer and in 1985 the first Conservative woman rabbi was ordained. Men and women now sit together in the synagogue and there is a constant effort to reconcile tradition with change.

An interesting offshoot of Conservative Judaism is Reconstructionism, which was instituted by Mordecai Kaplan (1881-1983). Kaplan was born in Lithuania, but emigrated with his family to the United States at the age of nine. For most of his career he was head of the Teachers' Training Institute at the Jewish Theological Seminary and, through that position, he exerted an enormous influence on generations of rabbis. Immensely learned in the Jewish tradition, he also studied the sociology of Durkheim, the biology of Darwin, the biblical criticism of Wellhausen, the psychology of religion of William James, the psychology of Freud and the political writings of Marx. As a result of his studies he came to the conclusion that Judaism should grow beyond traditional supernaturalism: as he put it, "Supernatural religion is the astrology and alchemy stage of religion." At the same time, he insisted that the traditional Jewish commandments are essential for the maintenance of Jewish communal life. In his most famous book, *Judaism as Civilization*, he argued that Judaism is a civilization whose focal point is the Law; thus Reconstructionists are radical in theology, but Orthodox in practice. Over the years a network of synagogues has been founded with a small but lively group of members.

Meanwhile 13 percent of Jewish households belong to the Reform movement. In general, Reform Jews are the most religiously radical and socially affluent of all the Jews of the United States. Traditionally their synagogues are known as temples; most of the service is in English rather than in Hebrew; men and women take an equal part in the proceedings, and many of the distinguishing marks of Judaism have been abandoned. Reform Jews do not generally observe the laws of ritual slaughter; they do not eat only kosher food; they drive their cars and use electricity on the Sabbath; neither the men nor the women feel obliged to cover their heads, and the use of the ritual bath on a regular basis is unknown. The basis of the American Reform movement was the Pittsburgh Platform of 1885, which denied the binding character of the laws of Moses, and only retained those customs which were perceived to aid spirituality. Another traditional characteristic of the Reform movement was its anti-Zionist stance; committed to life in America, and convinced that Judaism was a religion and not a tribal tradition, the reformers of the 19th century saw no need for a Jewish homeland.

All this changed after World War II, for the Holocaust persuaded even the most patriotic American Jew that the state of Israel was essential for the safety of the Jewish people. The movement has also become more conservative theologically: more Hebrew is now used in the services; head-coverings are generally worn in the temples; and increasingly circumcision for men and immersion in the ritual bath is demanded of potential converts. There is greater encouragement of home celebration, and there is a strong commitment to social action. The vast majority of converts to Judaism come in through the Reform movement. Unlike the Orthodox, who have no desire to proselytize, the non-Orthodox recognize that if Jews are to enjoy the full benefits of modern society, it is all too probable that young Jews will choose to marry outside the faith. In order to keep these people within the fold, the Reform movement in particular strongly encourages the gentile partner to convert to Judaism. However the Orthodox do not recognize these conversions as valid, and insist that the children of female converts to Reform Judaism are gentiles.

Only nine percent of the American-Jewish population belongs to an Orthodox congregation; this is the only branch of American Judaism that is growing. Orthodoxy maintains a differentiation between the roles of men and women; among the strictly Orthodox, marriage at a young age and large numbers of children are the norm. Within this group are included the various Hasidic sects – all disciples of different *rebbes*. Also included are the Modern Orthodox, and adherents of the movement started by Samson Raphael Hirsch in 19th-century Germany. Many modern Orthodox synagogues in the US are not very different from conservative synagogues, in that men and women sit together, and many members of the congregation do not lead an Orthodox lifestyle. However, women do not go up on the *bimah* (dais), and the members regard themselves as Orthodox.

In the past, Judaism was a unified structure. Until the beginning of the 19th century, all Jews accepted that the Law was given by God. Certainly there were differences of opinion: the Sadducees quarreled with the Pharisees, the Rabbanites with the Karaites, the Shabbateans with the Sceptics and the Hasidim with the Mitnaggedim. However, there was a certain unanimity among the Jewish people which has been destroyed by emancipation and secularism; even among those who choose to belong to a synagogue, not all accept that Judaism was divinely inspired. The divisions between the Orthodox, the Conservative and the Reform run very deep: it is no longer possible to speak of a single Jewish religious system.

The Threat of Secularism

In the past Jews were compelled by the gentile world to be a separate people. In many places they were forced to wear distinctive clothing; they were restricted to living in special areas, and they were educated in their own schools. In order to survive among their hostile neighbors, they had no alternative but to turn in on themselves for emotional and financial support. There was too much hatred, too many pogroms; it was not realistic to depend upon any one else; only from other Jews was there the assurance of help and understanding. Inevitably, the community organized its own self-help organizations and its own charities; it looked to the synagogue for spiritual sustenance and to the house of study for intellectual stimulation.

The price of peace is vigilance:
Israeli soldiers on Mt Hermon on
the Golan height above Syria.

Jews lived their whole lives within the community and had no desire to look beyond it; indeed, the threat of being rejected by family and friends was so great that even the most rebellious child could be kept in line. In those days Jews had their own world and there was no alternative mode of living.

In addition, traditional Jewish law kept people within the community. Jews may only eat kosher food; while they may eat any vegetable, they may only taste meat taken from animals that both chew the cud and have a cloven hoof (sheep and oxen qualify, while pigs and rabbits do not). The animal must be killed in a certain way: its throat must be cut in a single slash with a perfectly sharp blade; the blood must be drained away and the meat must be salted and washed before it is cooked. Butchery is a skilled business; furthermore, a kosher butcher must be a pious man who has studied his subject. The meat that is sold in the gentile market places is not acceptable. Birds can be eaten provided that they themselves do not live on carrion, but again they must be slaughtered in the proper manner. Fish is also a possibility, but only those which have fins and scales; shellfish of any kind are forbidden. In addition, there is a mysterious verse in the Pentateuch which forbids the seething (cooking) of a kid in its mother's milk, which the rabbis interpreted to mean that meat and milk foods may never be consumed together. A traditional Jewish household therefore has different areas in the kitchen for milk and meat foods; different saucepans, plates, dishpans, cutlery and dishcloths must also be used.

The effect of these rules is that Jews cannot eat in a gentile home or visit a gentile restaurant. It is not enough to order fish or a vegetarian meal, for the knives and forks will have been used for meat foods at some time and they will have all been washed together. Only food cooked by other pious Jews is safe, which means that the result of the Jewish food laws is to maintain a separation between the Jewish community and its neighbors. The laws of the Sabbath have very much the same consequence. Orthodox Jews will do no work from Friday evening until Saturday evening. They will not travel in their cars, because that would involve igniting a spark, breaking the law against kindling a fire. They will not write letters, because writing is classified as work; they will not speak on the telephone, and they will not conduct any form of business. This means that it is impossible for them to be employed in any enterprise that does work on a Saturday. Indeed, the reason why so many Jewish immigrants to the New World started their own business was to avoid working on the Sabbath.

Thus there are constraints within the Jewish legal system to keep the Jews a separate people, and there was hostility from outside the community which strengthened the resolve for apartness. In the old days, marriage to a gentile was unthinkable: it was the great sin; an enormous grief. On the rare occasions upon which it happened, parents would mourn for the erring child as if he or she had died. Although in any event opportunities for such marriages were almost nonexistent. All this changed with the Enlightenment and Jewish emancipation. Particularly in the New World, Jews wanted their children to take advantage of the many new opportunities offered: they wanted them to go to the best universities, to succeed in

Overleaf: Today's Israel is not an armed camp but a lively and colorful nation

business and to qualify for a profession. All too often religious scruples were not allowed to get in the way of these ambitions, perhaps resulting in a compromise: they would eat non-kosher food out, while maintaining a strictly kosher home; they would use their cars on the Sabbath, but only to see relations. In many cases the whole edifice gradually crumbled and many Jews began to lead lives which were indistinguishable from those of their gentile neighbors; they attended the same restaurants; they enjoyed the same entertainments; and they got to know each other as human beings.

The result was inevitable: an explosion in intermarriage. In the United States it is reckoned that about half the marriages celebrated today which involve Jews are intermarriages. The Reform movement in particular does its best to convert the non-Jewish partner, but very many young Jews feel no allegiance to the faith of their ancestors, for there is much in the old customs that is contrary to modern ways of thinking, the position of women being an obvious example.

Judaism has always been a religion with clearly defined roles for men and women; marriage and motherhood are the only acceptable destinies for a strictly Orthodox-Jewish girl. There is no equivalent to the Christian tradition of monasticism, where a woman can withdraw from the world and cultivate a private relationship with the Almighty; the duty of a Jewish woman is to marry a Jewish man and raise a bevy of Jewish children. Turning the pages of the *Encyclopaedia Judaica*, there are almost no female entries – women are merely remembered as the wives and mothers of male heroes. Inevitably, the feminist movement has not been happy with this treatment of women. A large proportion of the adult Jewish population, both male and female, are university graduates, and young women are as ambitious as young men for success in their careers. Among such an educated group, late marriage and, at most, two children are the norm; many choose never to marry. For many such young women, the traditional female Jewish role seems to hold few attractions.

There is also the problem of homosexuality; homosexual acts are regarded as an abomination in the Book of Leviticus. Homosexuality, if it existed in the community, was unrecognized. In the past, it was usual to arrange marriages for young people while they were still in their teens; despite their sexual orientation, young bridegrooms did their duty, and impregnated their wives. Again, all this has changed: today, most homosexual Jewish people are as ready to "come out" as their gentile counterparts. Some have retained their links with Judaism and in most major American cities there is at least one "gay congregation." But many homosexual Jews conclude that Judaism is not for them, and they cut all links with their roots.

Secularism must thus be seen as a great threat to the Jewish religion. Hitler murdered six million Jews but at least the same number are disappearing from the community through intermarriage or alternative lifestyles; the figures speak for themselves. The United States has the largest number of Jews in the world, but only 47 percent of those are affiliated with a synagogue; 53 percent hold themselves aloof.

Overleaf: Today's Israel is not an armed camp but a lively and colorful nation

The Future of Judaism

So what of the future of the Jewish faith and the Jewish people? In the first place, the Jewish state, the state of Israel, has never seemed so secure. The surrounding nations have acknowledged its existence; hands have been shaken, politicians embraced and treaties signed. Even the seemingly insoluble problem of the displaced Palestinian Arabs seems to be reaching some sort of solution through compromise. Israel continues to welcome Jewish settlers from all over the world. At present the main focus is on those from Russia, for the breakdown of the Soviet state has revealed all the latent anti-Semitism of the great Russian Empire. Jewish people are leaving their cities by the thousands, and many are choosing to make a new life for themselves in the Promised Land. In the future, persecution of Jews may occur elsewhere, although it seems unthinkable that another fascist government may come to power in Western Europe or in the United States. None-the-less, the future is unpredictable, and, as long as the Jewish state exists, Jews feel that they have a place of safety somewhere in the world.

However, the Jewish state is not free from religious conflict and despite the Orthodox control over matters of personal status, Israel is not a theocracy: many Israelis are completely nonreligious. There is pressure to introduce civil as well as religious marriage, and the Reform movement has established a foothold in the state and is campaigning vigorously for the right to marry and bury its adherents. The Orthodox, on the other hand, reject any form of pluralism: for them Judaism is Orthodoxy and pluralism is an anathema. It is hard to see how such profound religious conflicts in the Jewish state can be reconciled.

Meanwhile, the prognosis for Jewry outside Israel is gloomy. The birth rate of Diaspora Jews, with the notable exception of the strictly Orthodox, is dangerously low; intermarriage is rife; the attraction of assimilation into the gentile world is enormous. Some commentators believe that within a few generations, Judaism will only survive among the strictly Orthodox, who can be trusted to follow the ancient customs, to keep within their own communities, and to live a life out of tune with the manners and mores of the secular 21st century. But, as their coreligionists fall away, these people will become like the modern Karaites or Samaritans within Judaism, or the Amish or Mennonites within Christianity: they will be interesting subjects for anthropological theses, but they will be irrelevant to mainstream culture. Their assimilated Jewish and half-Jewish neighbors will have dim memories of a Jewish past, but will, like the Ten Lost Tribes, ultimately disappear from history.

Other commentators are not so pessimistic. They insist that, despite the strictly Orthodox, Judaism has, in fact, always been a pluralistic system. There have been constant intercommunity quarrels and, as the old saying goes, "Where there are four Jews, there are six opinions!" The heroes of Masada believed that they were the last of the Jewish people, but the rabbis managed to shake off the trauma of the destruction of the Jerusalem Temple and forged a new religious system centered round the Law and the synagogue. Through the whole mechanism of debate and scholarship,

Jewish law and culture have constantly adapted themselves to changing circumstances. There have been successful Jewish communities all over the world: each one has had individual characteristics, but ultimately all have been accepted within the bounds of Jewry. The optimists are encouraged by the constant stream of new recruits to the system that have been converted by the Reform movement. Many of these proselytes put Jews by birth to shame: they are committed to their new way of life; they bring up their children to be faithful Jews; and, increasingly, they are taking a prominent part in the administration of Jewish institutions. It is unfortunate that the Orthodox will not recognize their Jewishness, but no doubt this difficulty will be overcome in the future.

However, the situation today is different from the past: then Judaism was essentially a unified structure, embracing different interpretations of the Law. In this century, there has been unprecedented fragmentation. Most non-Orthodox Jews do not accept the divine authorship of the Law – many do not even believe in God. A large proportion of Diaspora Jewry have no religious affiliation whatsoever. On the one hand, the Progressives argue that Jewish law must adapt itself to take into account the insights of feminism, psychology and the sciences. On the other, the Orthodox maintain that the Law is perfect, and that no deviation is permitted. For the majority of Jews, the whole debate is irrelevant; they identify themselves as Jews, but they know little of the tradition, and they prefer to concentrate on the everyday business of making a living in a highly complex world.

In the second half of the 20th century, the community has had two focuses: the Holocaust, and the state of Israel. The Holocaust was a tragedy of such enormity that few can come to terms with it, and it convinced many that Jews can never be completely safe in the Diaspora. The state of Israel must therefore be supported with money, political lobbying, and unswerving commitment, to make sure that there is always a Jewish refuge. It is commonplace for present-day Jews to declare, "We are not religious, but we do support Israel!" For many Jews, God and the Law have been replaced in a very real sense by the Holocaust and the state of Israel. Most religious commentators believe that these two foci will not be enough to sustain the Jewish people in the future. Fifty years have passed since the dreadful days of Hitler's Germany. Despite the interest in such films as *Schindler's List* and the opening of Holocaust museums, inevitably the events lose their immediacy. In thirty years time, there will be no survivors left to give eye-witness accounts. Meanwhile, in other places in the world, appalling atrocities have occurred. Kurds have been murdered in Iraq; there has been 'ethnic cleansing' in the former Yugoslavia and there is a constant tribal warfare in central African countries. Despite scholarly attempts to demonstrate its unique status, the Holocaust will widely be perceived as one historical massacre among many.

At the same time, Israel has become increasingly self-supporting and correspondingly less willing to bow to outside opinion. Furthermore, the influx of Jewish immigrants from Arab lands and the growth of strict Orthodoxy has made the country seem increasingly foreign to the average, secularised Western Jew. As a result, most commentators believe that the next gener-

BELOW: Jerusalem Day is a joyous occasion for a proud, but still young nation.

ation of American and European Jews will feel less dedication than their parents to the rebuilding of the Promised Land.

The religious authorities, both Orthodox and Reform, are convinced that religious renewal is essential for the survival of Jewish civilization. They have accepted that their task is to present the beliefs of Abraham, Isaac and Jacob in a way that speaks to Jews today. The Jewish people have maintained their special identity for over three thousand years. If they are not to disappear from history, the argument runs, they must return to their religious roots. Only then can the Pillar of the Cloud, the Divine Presence, continue to guide the Chosen People through the wilderness of this world towards a glorious, but unknown future.

PHOTO CREDITS
The bulk of the photographs in this book were provided by Hanan Isachar except for those from the people and organisations listed below. The Author and Publisher acknowledge gratefully the assistance of all concerned.

ASAP
Nitsan Shorer 13. Sammy Arnison 17. David Rubinger 176, 177(T).
Jacob Raszemacher 10. Israel Talby 14(B), 15(B). W&CLA 177(B).

Egyptian Tourist Board
27.

David Eschel 178.

Irish Tourist Board
130(both) Brian Lynch.

Israel Government Tourist Office
5, 7(both), 15(T), 16, 17(B), 18(B), 20, 21, 25, 33, 35, 39, 44, 49, 68(both), 69, 71(B), 77, 81(T), 86(T), 88, 89, 92, 106, 107, 108(both), 112, 114, 115, 119(both), 126, 138(B), 156, 172.

Life File
123, 129, 163(all), 167 — Andrew Ward. 131(TLand B) Emma Lee. 131(TR), 155(B), Nigel Shuttleworth.

Sunburst Picture Library
161, 164(both).

Peter Waller 78.

INDEX

INDEX